KEEP
ON
KEEPING
ON

Other books by James W. Gilley

The Battle Is the Lord's

KEEP
ON
KEEPING
ON

ENCOURAGING STORIES
TO CARRY YOU THROUGH

JAMES W. GILLEY

Pacific Press® Publishing Association
Nampa, Idaho
Oshawa, Ontario, Canada
www.pacificpress.com

Copyright 2005 by
Pacific Press® Publishing Association
Printed in United States of America
All rights reserved

Book design by Dennis Ferree
Cover photo Alan Kearney/Getty Images

Additional copies of this book are available
by calling toll free 1-800-765-6955 or
by visiting http://www.adventistbookcenter.com.

Library of Congress Cataloging-in-Publication Data:

Gilley, James W., 1940-
Keep on keeping on : don't let the tough times deflate you/James
W. Gilley.
p. cm.
ISBN: 0-8163-2059-4
1. Christian life. 2. Suffering-Religious aspects-Christianity.
I. Title

BV4501.3.G555 2005
248.4-dc22   2004057330

05 06 07 08 09 · 5 4 3 2 1

DEDICATION AND ACKNOWLEDGMENTS

I'm dedicating this book . . . to my best friend and love of my life, my beautiful wife, Camille. As my friends are fond of pointing out, I definitely overachieved when I married you! . . . to my children in reverse order of their birth: Amy, John, Maryann, her husband, Kirk Krueger, and their children, Katie, Ben, Camille, Grace, and Carrie. James Jr., his wife, Pam, and their children, Chloe and James III . . . to my brothers: Ed, John, and Paul . . . to all my teachers for their love and patience—especially Ethel Jenkins Allaway, Sarah Martinez, and Harry Holder during my early years. During my Southwestern years: C. C. "Captain" Blackburn, Harold Lickey, Lawrence Scales, M. D. Lewis, and Altus Hayes (the business manager who kept letting me back in school even though I owed a lot of money!). At Andrews University: Don Jacobsen, Bruce Johnston, and Ivan Blazen, who finally gave me a passing grade in Greek!

. . . to some special pastors, evangelists, and leaders: Fordyce Detamore, Ben Leach, E. E. Cleveland, Roger Holley, Kenneth Cox, Charles Bradford, Neal Wilson, Bob Folkenberg, Dale Brusett, H. M. S. Richards, Jr., Dick and Henry Barron—especially Henry, who, as a young pastor, greatly influenced me during my teenage years. He became my loyal friend and eventually copastor in Arlington! To my former bosses: Merle Mills, Russell Adams, Lowell Bock, Bill May, Don Aalborg, and Bob Wood, and my current boss, Don Schneider, and his North American Division team, with which I have the privilege of working.

. . . to all those with whom I have worked closely during the years. In evangelism: Gene and Lucy Fletcher, Spencer and Mary Alice Gordon, Ray Hubbartt, David Peterson, Carl Phipps, and Michael Cuilla. In business: the entire MTES team, Kathy Smith and three of the finest gentlemen I've ever known: L. H. Coleman, Harvey Brown, and Dean Harrison.

In Arlington, Texas: Henry Barron, Bill and Connie Perryman, Howard and Selma Conley, Myron Voegle, Mike Tucker, and the entire membership of the greatest congregation in the world! In Ukraine: N. A. Zhukaluk, Leonid Drach, Galena Gritsuk, Ivan Kosovan, and my friend, translator, and partner in preaching, Valery Tchunkovski. At the Arkansas-Louisiana Conference in Shreveport: Art Nelson, Steve Orian, Don Upson, Don Hevener, Eddie Canales, Charles Dart, Tibor Shelley, Bonnie Hernandez, the entire office staff, and the pastors and members of the Arkansas-Louisiana Conference, who showed faith in me and were great to work with for those seven fantastic years! . . . to Mike and Rhonda Tomblinson, Rudy Hein, Ross Sawyer, Don Fortner, John Taylor, and Dexter Le Blanc, some of whom I didn't even know at the time that they worked so hard along with others to have me reinstated as president of the Arkansas-Louisiana Conference. I'm afraid that without these brave people, my ministry would have come to a grinding halt! . . . to the presidents' council of the Southwestern Union, with whom I enjoyed working for so many years: Max Trevino, Cyril Miller, Ralph Orduno, Bob Lister, Bill Wright, Steve Gifford, Rodney Grove, Jim Stevens, Sam Green, Buford Griffin, Walter Wright, and Deryl Knutson.

. . . to all of my very many friends, but especially to Dan Buckingham, Gary Grimes, Carl Markstrom, Vern Carner, Jim Root, Bill Lingo, Harold Collum, Herman Harp, Jim Ripley, and all those friends listed previously with whom I have studied or worked. And to a host of others who will be mad at me for not including them specifically—but probably not as many as will be mad because I *have* put them on the list!

I especially wish to thank Betty Trevino for editing the first draft; my daughters, Amy and Maryann, and Don Jacobsen, Alvin Kibble, Kermit Netteberg, and other friends for reading my manuscript and offering suggestions and encouragement; and Carolyn Adams for her tireless labor in preparing this book for print. I greatly appreciate the encouragement of my book editor, Tim Lale, and the freedom he has given me to tell it like it is—or at least as I saw it!

And most of all, I want to thank my Lord and Savior Jesus Christ, who has never given up on me and to whom I owe everything. He has taught me that He can use pain, disappointment, failure, and defeat as tools to mold our characters into a closer representation of His perfection.

TABLE OF CONTENTS

Introduction

"There are enough bad books on the market already!"

I didn't originate that line; Peter Marshall did. Not the game show host, but the great Presbyterian orator and pastor who was also chaplain of the U.S. Senate and died of a heart attack at a tragically young age.

I used Marshall's words to respond to Dale Galusha and Jerry Thomas when they cornered me at an Adventist Laymen's Services and Industries (ASI) convention and asked me to write a book for Pacific Press. *Who would read it?* I wondered. Evidently someone did, because soon after my first book was published, Tim Lale, successor to Jerry Thomas, sat down in my cramped office at the General Conference and asked me to write another book!

I had titled my first book *Keep On Keeping On* because the first and last chapters are based on a sermon by that title that I have preached hundreds of times throughout the U.S. and Ukraine. However, a book committee at Pacific Press decided to use a different title and chose *The Battle Is the Lord's,* the title of another chapter. When I asked them why they chose not to keep the title I had suggested, they responded that they didn't feel an old cowboy motto was spiritual enough to suit the subject matter.

I accepted that explanation, but later the chairman of the committee saw me at a conference where I was speaking in the Northwest. After hearing my signature sermon, he admitted, "We should have gone with that title." So, now I'm giving Pacific Press one more chance! However, if you hear me preach the sermon "Keep On Keeping On" and you want the material I present in it, you will have to obtain a copy of *The Battle Is the Lord's*. It's available at your local Adventist Book Center, from adventistbookcenter.com, or from Amazon.com.

Only one chapter in this book, "When You Feel Like Throwing In the Towel," is based on any sermon I have ever preached. And while a couple of the experiences I share in this book have been told publicly before, most have not. I wrote this book in part while sitting comfortably at a computer. But most often, I wrote it in longhand on a legal pad while trying to shut out the noise of a crowded airplane or while waiting in an airport terminal for a delayed plane. If you want a book on trials and tribulations, I can assure you any frequent flyer is qualified to write one!

This book is not devotional reading. There's no replacing the Bible for that. My wife rises early for her devotions and reads a different translation each year. I do a combination of reading and listening to Alexander Scourby read the old King James Version, which I love. If your mind wanders, try doing both at the same time. Let Scourby pace you and pronounce the difficult words for you. Take it in shorter sessions. You may also want to pause the tape or CD at the end of a chapter and write your thoughts in a notebook. You can mark texts that are especially encouraging. You might also consider copying those texts in a notebook for times when you need your spirits lifted.

Fordyce Detamore, one of my many mentors, said that he kept a loose-leaf notebook filled with texts, poems, articles, lyrics, and anything else he found encouraging. When discouragement or depression came (which he battled all of his life), he would read something uplifting from that notebook. Similarly, I copy my favorite inspirational songs on a tape or burn them on a CD. I find these especially helpful when I need extra encouragement.

Most of my inspirational music is religious. I never tire of hearing Herman Harp and Marvin Ponder sing "Unmerited Favor." However, songs like "To Dream the Impossible Dream" from *The Man of La Mancha*, "Climb Every Mountain" from *The Sound of Music*, and even Louis Armstrong's "What a Wonderful World" lift me up too. Unfortunately, such songs are few and far between! If you're fighting discouragement or depression, one of the things you should note is the kind of music you've been listening to. If the lyrics are down in the dumps, no wonder you're depressed!

This book is certainly not autobiographical, although it does contain numerous experiences from my life. Arthur and Theresa Beem, along with their children, were visiting our home in the Washington, D.C., area. I don't remember what particular experience I was sharing with them as we chatted one evening after enjoying a wonderful meal from "Camille's Kitchen." But Theresa, whom I have known all her life, suggested I write down some of my stories as an encouragement to others. Even though reliving some of these experiences and writing them down revived some of the original pain, it was also therapeutic and spiritually strengthening. When I finally got started, I wrote what became chapter two. I showed it to Tim Lale, and he said, "Send us more." So if you don't like this book, now you know the people you should blame. Contact me, and I'll be happy to give you their addresses!

On a more serious note, it is truly my desire that this book will encourage you and that it will inspire you never to give up on life or our Lord. It is not a theological discourse, so if you find yourself brooding over deep concepts, they didn't come from me! This is meant to be easy, light reading to encourage you when you are facing difficult times. Perhaps I should have called it *Pepto-Bismol for the Soul* or *Chickett Soup for the Soul*—though I guess something like the last one is already out there! Sometimes you'll laugh while reading this. I hope it doesn't make you cry, but I must confess that I did a couple of times as I wrote it.

Those who travel by plane know the old saying "Any landing you can walk away from is a good landing." I've had some rough rides and some very rough landings in my life, but so far, with the Lord's help, I've always been able to walk away. And while my life has been more difficult than some, it has been a cakewalk when compared to others. I'm sure that the Lord never allows more difficulties in life than He gives us the grace to handle. It is only through Him that I can face each day and each challenge.

Introduction

One day there will be a landing that I won't be able to walk away from, but I have every confidence that He will be there to carry me in His loving arms. Until then, I am determined to keep on keeping on with Jesus, holding on to Him and relying on Him for absolutely everything!

CHAPTER ONE

WHEN BAD THINGS HAPPEN

*W*hy in the world do all these things have to happen to me? I am sure that John must have asked this question. John was no ordinary human being. After all, an angel announced his birth! His mission had been appointed before his birth, and his lifestyle—even down to the details of what he would and wouldn't eat and drink—had been equally foreordained. Since his job was to announce the coming of the Messiah, he was by far the most popular person in all of Israel. God had chosen him, yet there he sat in jail.

Things looked bleak for John. One day by the Jordan River, John had announced the Messiah, and now *Jesus* was the name on everyone's lips. John had known he was to decrease in popularity, but he wasn't prepared to disappear from the scene altogether! Certainly there must be a place for him, perhaps a number two spot, even if that meant being a disciple or simply a witness to the miracles that he imagined this Messiah would perform.

But a lonely prison cell?

Is Jesus truly the Messiah, John began to question, *or is there to be another?* John sent his followers to talk to Jesus. Perhaps his real motive was to make sure Jesus knew that he was in prison. He had to wonder why Jesus didn't do something about his situation. Later, Jesus sent angels to release some of His disciples from prison. Couldn't he have done the same for John? Couldn't He at least visit John? After all, hadn't Jesus said that God's children should visit prisoners? Yet John was waiting alone!

Waiting always seems to be the most trying part of trials, doesn't it? However, the fact that Jesus left John in jail didn't mean that Jesus didn't love him! The fact that John was executed in a degrading way didn't mean that Jesus didn't care! The fact that He didn't rescue John or even pay him a comforting visit didn't mean that John had sinned or was rejected. Jesus made that clear when He said, "There was not greater born of a woman than John."

Lately, too many people have adopted the philosophy that if you are a Christian, God will place a hedge of protection around you. You and your children will be safe. You will always be protected, and everything will work out for your benefit. You will be rich and successful in everything you do. Tell that to John the Baptist.

While you're at it, tell it to Job. Tell it to Peter as he's crucified upside down. Tell it to John the Beloved, exiled on the Isle of Patmos. Tell it to Paul while he's flogged five times with thirty-nine lashes, beaten with rods three times, shipwrecked three times, and spends a day clinging to wreckage tossed about the open sea. Tell it to him while he's being stoned and left for dead.

Consider Paul. Life had probably been pretty smooth for Paul up until his conversion. He was minding his own business—the persecution business—when a bright light from heaven blinded him and God called him to be an apostle. You would think things would get easier from that point on. However, instead of receiving a wall of protection when he became a Christian, he struggled through trial after trial.

Paul didn't get a safety net when he was converted. Neither did I; and I suspect you didn't either. Certainly, I've received more blessings than I deserved, and I'm thankful for the protection I have received. But like you, I also know what it is like to run into a brick wall. To have the proverbial rug pulled out from under me. To have life blow up in my face. The apostle Paul said, "We are hard pressed on every side, but not crushed; perplexed, but not in despair; persecuted, but not abandoned; struck down, but not destroyed" (2 Corinthians 4:8, 9, NIV).

You will be tempted over and over to quit—to give up believing in Christ, relying on Him, and trusting Him. You'll be tempted to quit your job, to abandon your marriage, and to give up on life in general. Sometimes it is difficult for us to realize that the fact that we fail doesn't mean we're failures. And the fact that we lose doesn't mean we're losers. We become failures and losers only if we become quitters!

Look at Abraham Lincoln. Through most of his life, he was a failure—a miserable, wretched, repeated, everlasting failure! As a young man, he ran for the state legislature and was overwhelmingly defeated. He then went into business, failed completely, and spent the next seventeen years paying his debts and the debts of his irresponsible partner.

He proposed to a beautiful and loving girl. She died. Later, he married a woman whose mental condition was a continual burden to him—a veritable thorn in the flesh. He decided to run for Congress and was swamped. After that, he tried to get an appointment to the United States Land Office and was turned down. He decided he ought to run for the United States Senate and once again was pounded into the ground.

After all these defeats, one might think he would decide that perhaps he was aiming too high and should settle for a more modest attainment. Instead, he decided to run for vice president of the United States! He was defeated once more. Finally, he ran for the presidency of the United States. Of course, he was victorious, and now he's known as one of the greatest men in the history of the world.

When we listen to the litany of losing that shadowed the background of a man who so wonderfully succeeded in the end, are we not ashamed at the number of times we have given up? The essence of losers is that they quit. Even though Abraham Lincoln was defeated time after time, he was never a loser because he never quit.

Your life may be like that. You may have failed the Lord, your family, your friends, and even those with whom you work. But that does not make you a failure! You may have lost some battles, even with yourself and with "the sin that so easily besets you." You may have little or no self-control, but that doesn't mean you've lost the war, not as long as you never quit surrendering yourself to Jesus. If you keep on keeping on, I promise you that you will succeed in the long run.

We are a success-oriented people. There are the dot-com billionaires with their million-dollar mansions and their "toys," like private jets and professional ball teams. Society calls them successful. But I wonder who will be thought of as a success in God's kingdom. Probably no one the world calls a success! I don't picture the Lord recognizing the rich and famous. Instead, I imagine Him praising people whom we have never heard of, who have stood firm and trusted Him despite all the trials that have come their way.

My study of the Word leads me to believe that most of the struggles we face come from someone other than the Lord. I don't think He shipwrecked Paul and had him beaten and then stoned. I believe that Paul was a child of God, and God is not a child abuser. He doesn't abuse you, me, or any of His children. A long time ago, the Lord tried to tell Adam and Eve what sin would bring to this world, but they chose to believe the lies of a talking snake instead. You and I sometimes believe that same snake, Satan, as he blames what he has done to the world on a loving God!

While God may not cause the problems we face, I *do* believe that when we trust Him through these trials, He develops our character to be more like His. What Satan has meant to destroy us, God uses to strengthen us.

Ironic, isn't it? We must not miss the blessing hidden in even the most difficult trial. We must continue on toward the finish line of life even when we trip and fall from time to time.

Amazingly, in time, you may see the trials you've faced as the highlights of your life. You may realize that trusting God in these difficulties has increased your faith, not in yourself, but in Him. You may see that your trust has developed so much that you are ready to echo Job, "Though He slay me, yet will I trust Him" (Job 13:15, NKJV).

Not only is God with you in the good times, when everything is beautiful and easy, but He's also there during the dark times. Perhaps He's never closer than in those difficult moments! Do you remember the poem "Footprints in the Sand"? That poem pictures a man who sees two sets of footprints tracing through the smooth parts of his life. Then he notices that in the difficult stretches, there's only one set of footprints. Feeling puzzled and forsaken, he asks the Lord, "Where were You when I really needed You?" The Lord answers, "Those are My footprints. I was carrying you."

The apostle Paul said, "I have fought a good fight, I have finished my course, I have kept the faith: Henceforth there is laid up for me a crown of righteousness" (I Tim. 4:7, 8, KJV). That, my friend, is true for you and for me.

So, keep on keeping on when life throws its most difficult trials your way.

CHAPTER TWO

WHEN YOU WANT TO RUN AWAY FROM IT ALL

When I was a teenager, my family lived in Dallas. But during most of my early years, we lived in Tyler, Texas. My best friends, especially during the years before my twelfth birthday, were Dan Buckingham, Jimmy Don McCoy, and George Seaberry, whom we called Seabiscuit after the famous racehorse. These were the only other boys my age who attended the little church school located in a back room of the church on Berta Street. Even after the school closed and we had all gone different directions to the public schools that were near our homes, we remained friends and saw one another at least each week at church.

George was a careful and cautious person by nature. He always obeyed his parents and was the kind of son that all parents wish they had. For that reason, I don't have any good stories to tell about him! The other two were very adventurous, and I'm sure that any unbiased observer would have made the same assessment of me.

As babies under a year old, Dan and I, who were only a month apart, had kicked the slats out of our playpen together. Well, at least, we played together. George was about a year older than Dan and I, and Jimmy Don was another year older.

Jimmy Don was a Huck Finn–type of person. He was ready for any adventure. It was with him that I got into the most trouble. I suppose that's why Dad didn't like it when I spent time with him. I thought Dad was being unfair.

Jimmy Don was also a real daredevil. The viaduct over the rail yards in Tyler had cement rails. One day I saw Jimmy Don put his bike on that rail and ride it the full length of the bridge. Traffic stopped to watch him, the drivers yelling for him to get off there, but he never slowed.

Once we slipped up on a hobo camp under the viaduct. We watched the men as they talked around the campfire and shared their brew. When they discovered we were spying on them, they became upset and began to chase us. I was just sure that they were planning on putting us in their pot as the next course, so I ran with all my might. When I looked back to see if they were gaining, I tripped over a hobo who was sleeping on the ground away from the rest of the group. I went sprawling. The hobo was as surprised as I was, but I recovered quickly, and none of those hobos had a ghost of a chance of catching me, now that I was really scared.

On one occasion when Jimmy Don was visiting me, we threw rocks at a train. When the train passed, we decided to use cars as our targets, with the hubcaps as bull's eyes. We both threw at a passing car, and one of us—I'm not sure which one, probably me—had poor aim. So, one rock sailed high and broke a window on the passenger side of the car.

My dad was painting our house at the time. The driver of the car called him down from the ladder and told him what happened, and my dad had to pay for the window. He told me he was going to take the money out of my hide, and he did.

Dad sold that house, and we moved down the road to the country. Jimmy Don came and visited me there too. We'd learned our lesson about throwing rocks, but one day when we were bored, we found something better to throw—some eggs that one of our chickens had laid in a nest out in a field. Evidently, the hen was trying to hatch some baby chicks, but we didn't have a rooster, so all the eggs did was rot.

The highway ran over a creek on a small bridge, and our property extended along both sides of the highway. Jimmy Don hid below the bridge on one side of the highway, and I did the same on the other. As an unsuspecting car came along the road, we both lobbed our rotten-egg "hand grenades" over the edge of the bridge, hitting the car from both sides.

The driver had just had his car washed, and he and the young woman with him were going somewhere to eat and had dressed up for the occasion. At that time, cars didn't have air conditioning, so they had their windows were open. One egg splattered them both, and the other landed on the hood of the car, splattering the windshield.

Jimmy Don and I ran to a gully and hid. As we watched, the car turned around and made its way to my house—the only one around. We were caught!

Dad asked the man to go to the service station, have his car washed, and put it on his account. He told him to do the same at the cleaners we used. Then he found us, drove Jimmy Don home, and took the entire cost out of my hide again!

Many times when my dad was about to punish me, he would say, "Son, this hurts me more than it does you." I often wanted to reply, "Then why not save us both a lot of pain and not do it!" But a wisecrack like that would have really brought the wrath down. Later, as a parent, trying to raise my children to obey, I knew what he meant. It hurts us when we see our children doing things that are harmful to them and to others.

Jimmy Don wasn't afraid of anything or anyone. During my senior year in academy, I got a call to come to Tyler. Jimmy Don had been involved in a terrible, one-car accident and was dead. I will always miss my friend.

Dan Buckingham was my closest friend. He'd been born with a handicap: His right arm was withered. His parents took him to the Scottish Rite Hospital for surgery several times during his childhood. I'm certainly no fan of any of the secret organizations, but I appreciate the fact that this group did not charge Dan's parents a dime for those surgeries. The doctors donated their time. The surgeries gave Dan more use of his arm, though not anywhere near complete use.

When Dan would go for a surgery, he and his mother would travel to Dallas by Trailways bus. He told me the hospital staff would take them into an auditorium filled with about five hundred people—

kids and parents. There they would wait until his name was called. Then they would go into an examination room to see the doctor. Dan said that if the doctor—his was a Dr. Carroll—decided to do surgery, he would be taken from his mother right to the room where he was prepped for the surgery.

After their surgeries, the young patients were put in a ward of twenty-four kids. The hospital allowed visitation only during a two-hour period on Sunday afternoons. Dan's mom lived in Tyler, a hundred miles away, and didn't have the money to come for a visit every week, so his uncle and aunt would visit him each Sunday. He'd have to stay for a month to six weeks each time he went to the hospital; that allowed time for the surgery, healing, and the beginning of rehab. All this time, Dan was away from his parents. He says that's why he became so independent—though I think that, mostly, he was born that way!

I worried about Dan when he went for these surgeries, but he always reassured me. "I'll fight death!" he would say in a very loud voice and with conviction. I was sure that he would, and was always glad to see him come home "victorious over death one more time."

I have more respect for Dan than for anyone else I have ever known. He had—and still has—one of the greatest "spirits" I've ever seen in anyone. His handicap did not slow him one bit. My respect for him began to grow the first time he outran me. I had always won when we had raced, but then one day he inched me out. I demanded a rematch. He agreed—and beat me even worse! I never could catch him again. He had blinding speed.

Unless I was scared, my speed was average. In junior high, I tried out for the track team, and the coach attempted to find a place for me. Sonny Haley was the fastest man on the team, and we were friends. One Halloween we were out trick-or-treating. When the people at one house weren't very generous, we decided to aggravate them by knocking on the door and hiding to watch. We bothered the man so much he decided to scare us. As we walked up on the porch to knock, he threw open the door and pointed a shotgun at us. We both turned and ran, and I got so far ahead of Sonny that he started shouting for me to wait for him! The next day at track practice, Sonny told the coach he was sure I was the fastest runner in the school. He said that if the coach would just point a shotgun at me, he'd see that was true!

I might have even outrun Dan that night, but I doubt it. A few years later, we went by the high school, and the star sprinter from the track team, who'd won the state championship, was working out. Dan challenged him to a race and beat him twice. Dan was in street clothes and barefooted. The runner, in track shoes and running shorts, walked away shaking his head. I knew how he felt. The same thing happened to me in the fourth grade!

I became very interested in baseball the summer after I finished fifth grade. Tyler started a Little League baseball program that year, and I was in the first league they organized. The team I joined elected Mack Hickman and me captains. I'm sure that if the kids had ever seen me play baseball, they wouldn't have elected me.

At first, the rules were interpreted to mean that no adult could even coach us, so for the first few games we ran the team ourselves. We named our team the Apaches. Mack said he was going to be the pitcher. I liked wearing all the catcher's gear, so I said that I would play that position.

In the first inning, we found out that Mack Hickman could really pitch. He struck out the first three batters! However, I couldn't catch. I dropped every pitch. Of course, the runners ran on the third missed strike, and the bases were quickly loaded with no outs. So, Mack and I conferred on the mound. He was furious with me, and so were all the other players on our team. The shortstop said he could do better, and we traded places.

The next three batters hit the ball. Of course, each time, they hit it directly to me. All three balls went between my legs. At that point, the other team had scored three runs, and the bases were still loaded. Our team had only nine players, so they couldn't bench me. Instead, they sent me to center field and brought the center fielder in to play shortstop. And—you guessed it—the next batter hit the ball to center field, and my baseball career was dangerously near finished. I completed the game and the season in right field. Everyone prayed that no one would hit the ball there.

Mack's father had become our coach. What a patient and dedicated father he was to practice with us after working hard all day at his job! He was also a good coach and developed us into a winning team. Mr. Hickman knew that I was not a good player and was hurting the team. After the season was over, he told me, in a kind but firm way, that there would not be a place on the team for me the next season.

His words really broke my heart, though I knew his decision was justified. However, I determined I would become good enough to make the team the next year. I worked on baseball all winter long. Even when it was cold, I would throw a ball against a concrete step in the garage, learning to field grounders. My brother Ed, seeing my determination to improve, would hit fly balls to me by the hour out in the street next to our house.

When spring came and the Apaches began to practice, I showed up on the field. Mr. Hickman ordered me to leave, but I begged him for a tryout. Some of the other players had played with me earlier, and they appealed to him to give me a chance. He quickly saw I wasn't the same player he had put up with last summer, and I was back on the team. I had the best batting average on the team that year, and the coaches chose me as the most improved player in the league. At that point, baseball became a very important part of my life.

A couple seasons after I started playing Little League baseball, I was happy to hear that my friend Dan was playing in another league across town. I went to see him play his first game. Even with his handicap, Dan was a very good player. We had played a lot of sandlot ball together, and he had learned to catch the ball with the glove on his good left hand and, in one motion, remove the ball, grasp the glove with his withered right hand, and throw the ball to make the play.

As the game was starting, I heard one of the coaches tell the players on the opposing team that if they were safe at first base on a close play and the ball was thrown to Dan, they should keep running to second base, because they would reach it safely by the time Dan got the ball out of his glove. I was really upset that some coach would try to take advantage of a young man's handicap, but

I smiled quietly to myself because I knew Dan better than they did.

One of the first batters hit a slow grounder to third. The throw to first was late, and the batter rounded the base safely and headed toward second, following his coach's command. Dan was confused for a second, but he quickly recovered and threw the runner out as he neared second. The next batter did almost the same thing, and Dan threw him out so quickly that the opposing team never tried that tactic again! Dan became one of the best ballplayers I've ever played with, and I was proud of my ol' buddy.

I'll never forget that night—not only because Dan played so well but also because of what happened when I got home. I was hungry, so I ate a peanut-butter sandwich and drank a glass of tomato juice. Before morning, I woke up very sick to my stomach, vomited a number of times, and ended up in the hospital, where I had an emergency appendectomy. I still like peanut butter, and I still like tomato juice, but there is no way I could ever again have the two together!

We were still living in Tyler when I was about eleven years old. Sometimes kids get crazy ideas. I don't remember who came up with this one, but I believe it was Jimmy Don. I know that at least he gave us our destination. He'd read an ad in a magazine from a ranch out west that was advertising their need for working cowboys. I'd grown up around horses and knew a little about cattle. Dan knew a lot about both, and Jimmy Don could do anything.

We felt our parents were mistreating us. I was being treated much better than I deserved, but I'd begun to watch for any slight whatsoever, and then I magnified it out of its true proportion. Dan was doing the same. Jimmy Don really did have a very difficult home life; a few months after this incident, his folks divorced. It was the adventure that attracted Dan's and my attention. The three of us had decided that we would go out west and work on that ranch. The only way we could do that was to run away from home. (We'd invited George to go, but he was too wise and declined!)

I had $140 in a checking account in a bank in town. I'd purchased a calf from a dairy for a few dollars and fed it with a bottle until it could graze on its own. Dad had let me open the checking account with the proceeds of the sale of my calf. Mom had protested, but Dad thought it would teach me to manage money. Dad arranged for me to cash my checks at a convenience store down the street from his awning shop, because no one else would take a check from a kid. I had cashed small checks at that store and was quite sure the owner would cash a big check for me. So it was our plan that I would finance the trip, which we would make on our bicycles.

We planned to leave Sabbath morning. Our church services were in the afternoon, and frequently, some group or other met in the morning to hand out Bible-course enrollment cards or literature. The three of us often helped so that we could be together. So, we made doing mission work our cover story, but we rendezvoused instead at the Fun Forest swimming pool. Then we went to the convenience store to cash a check, because I'd had no opportunity to do so before. There we discovered that Dad had put a five-dollar limit on my check cashing. I argued with the owner that I needed more this time, and he finally allowed me to cash a six-dollar check. The meager funds threw a big wrinkle into things, but I thought we could still make it. Besides, we would have big-paying jobs soon!

So, with our sleeping bags and a few other items tied on the back of our bikes, we started up the road. Whenever we saw a police car, we would hide under a bridge. We thought for sure our folks had missed us and would be looking for us by now. We were also pretty sure they would call the police and sheriff's departments when they figured out that we were gone. We were right.

We spent so much time hiding that it took us all day to make it to Edom, a little town about twenty miles west of Tyler. There I saw my older brother, John, drive by in the family car. We had hidden, and my partners didn't think he'd seen us, but I knew he had and was just acting as if he hadn't. I was also tired of being a runaway, and home was starting to sound good. So I went to a pay phone and called home, collect.

Dad hesitated for a second when the operator asked if he would accept the call. Then he said Yes. I told him where we were and asked him to come in the pickup so we could bring the bikes back. He mumbled something like, "I should make you ride your bike back," but he came, and we were glad to see him.

We dropped Jimmy Don off near his house. He said later that no one acted as if they'd missed him or even said anything to him about where he'd been. Dan's folks had a disagreement over what his punishment should be, so he really lucked out—he received none. My dad took me into the bedroom, took off his belt, and gave me the hardest whipping I'd ever had in my life, all the time saying, "So, we're not good enough to you around here!" I couldn't tell if he wanted me to say yes or no. When it was all over and I thought about it, I realized that this was his way of saying that he loved me and that he wanted me to turn out to be a good, upstanding citizen.

I learned a lot that day. The biggest lesson was that when you try to run away, for whatever reason, it's most likely not going to work out for the best. Face the challenges of life head on. I also learned that the opportunities near home are probably much better than those we imagine wait for us somewhere else.

When you feel like running away from it all, don't! Keep on keeping on. A brighter day is coming, I guarantee it!

CHAPTER THREE

WHEN YOU MAKE A BAD CHOICE

Like most teenagers, I wanted my own car. Until I got one, my standard mode of travel was with my thumb. For the most part, I was lucky at catching good rides. For instance, my friend Nick Turman's brother, Buddy, who was a heavyweight boxer, was to make an appearance in Dallas with Audie Murphy, the famous war hero of World War II who had become an actor. The car Buddy was traveling in was packed with big shots. So we told him we would hitchhike from Tyler to Dallas, a distance of about a hundred miles, and see him there.

A few minutes after he left us, we caught a ride with Sam Trant, an oilman who was well known in the community. He didn't know us on sight, but he knew our families. His son Mike had played football with our older brothers.

Mr. Trant asked us where we were going. When we said, "Dallas," he asked, "Do you mind flying?" We said No, thinking he was talking about driving fast. But a few miles down the road, he turned into an airport, and I took my first flight in a plane. We actually beat Buddy and his entourage to the place where Audie Murphy was to appear, much to their surprise.

This experience opened a new horizon for me—a new mode of travel. Sometimes instead of heading for the highway, I'd head for an airport, hang around the terminal, and talk to the pilots until I found one who was headed in the direction I wanted to travel. On long

trips, that worked really well because many times the pilots were traveling alone and enjoyed the company.

Most of the time, however, I was making short trips, such as from
Keene, where Southwestern was located, fifty or so miles to Dallas,
where my parents lived. I learned the hard way not to take every ride
that came along. If I saw something I didn't like, I would make some
excuse and walk away.

One day I had a funny feeling about a man but decided to chance
riding with him anyway. When I got in the car and closed the door,
the old timer moved his right hand to reveal a revolver lying on the
seat. "Don't try anything, young man, or I'll blow your head off," he
said gruffly. I said I didn't intend to do anything to hurt him and
then told him all the good things about myself that I could think of
in an attempt to alleviate his fears. However, nothing seemed to make
him relax.

Eventually, I suggested that if he picked up anyone else, he
shouldn't keep his gun on the seat between them, as the criminal
could get to the gun as quickly as or quicker than he could. He said
that was impossible, so I reached over and grabbed the gun. He nearly
wrecked the car. Then he said that I was merely lucky, that I had
caught him by surprise. I gave him the gun, and he put it in the same
place. I immediately grabbed the gun again. "You fooled me!" he said.
I replied that I was sure no crook would give him a warning and that
he should really keep the gun over on the other side, by the door.
"But I'm right handed," he protested, "and there's no way you could
do that again." I promptly did, and he finally moved the gun, and we
had a good ride the rest of the way!

Many of my trips did not turn out so well, though, and I was tired
of having to do battle with the drunks, sex perverts, reckless drivers,
and just plain nutty people who picked me up. So, I wanted a car of
my own.

However, my first car proved to me that having a car wasn't necessarily wonderful either. I'd found a car that looked great to me. My
dad checked it over and recommended that I not buy it. But I wanted
it—it was a Dodge convertible! On my first trip in that car, I drove
to Texas City, Texas, where I worked as tent master for the Barron

brothers' evangelistic team. During the day I would sell books, and at night I would sleep in the tent to protect it. I slept so soundly that a thief could have carried off the whole place and I would never have known it! Dick and Henry Barron were great friends and were a big part of my life during that particular time.

When the summer was over, I started for Dallas, going through Houston so that I could stay on the "good" roads. On the way I thought, *I'll pick up a hitchhiker as payback for the rides nice people have given me.* So I picked out a clean-cut young man and offered him a ride. Shortly thereafter, I had a flat tire. Of course, when I changed the tire, I no longer had a spare. So I stopped at the next filling station and bought one—the cheapest one they had, which cost about a dollar.

A few miles down the road I had another flat, so I repeated the process. When it happened a third time, my hitchhiker grabbed his bag and said, "I'm sorry, I don't have time for this," and walked away. I kept hoping I would pass him somewhere on the road and could toot my horn as I went by, but I never had that privilege. I had two more flats before I reached Dallas and finally realized that I had to buy something better than trash-heap tires if I wanted to keep my car on the road!

Now I had transportation back and forth to school. The only problem was that I forgot to ask the school if I could have a car! The college students could bring cars and use them within limits, but the academy students weren't supposed to. So I decided not to say anything about the car. I planned to just park it in the lot and play dumb if anyone asked whose it was.

There's always a "snitch" around, though, trying to get in good with the dean, and soon Dean Basham was knocking on the door of my room and asking me about the car in the lot. I offered to give him the keys, but he said that wouldn't work because people always had extra keys. So, he told me to take the car home that weekend.

That was good because it wasn't a leave weekend. It meant I would get an extra weekend at home—always a welcome thing. I did take the car home, but I couldn't find a way back to school, so I drove the car back again.

A few days later, the dean saw me and said, "I thought I told you to take that car home."

I realized by the way he said it that he didn't know I had taken it home, so I said, "I'll take it this weekend, Dean."

He said, "Make sure you do."

I took it home that weekend, planning to ride back to school with a friend. However, my friend didn't show up, so I had to drive the car back to school again. This time the dean was upset and called me into his office. "I thought I told you to take that car home," he said, almost angrily.

"You did, Dean, but you didn't tell me not to bring it back," I said with a straight face.

The dean nearly burst a vein. "You take that car home this weekend and leave it there," he yelled at me.

I did—but in the process I'd gotten three trips home and three weekends of Mom's good home cooking instead of just one! However, sometimes the choices I made came back to bite me. For instance, there was the watermelon incident with the Turman boys.

I enjoyed spending time at the Turmans' house out in the country near Noonday, Texas, about ten miles from Tyler. Before we moved to Dallas, it was like my second home. There were eleven children in the family: nine boys and two girls. When I knew the family, both of the girls and four of the boys had grown up and were no longer living at home, but five of the boys were there most of the time. In the order of their ages, the five living at home were Buddy, Joe, Chester, Larry, and Nick.

The Turman boys were all pretty good guys—law-abiding and honest. They might do something like sneak into a "picture show" without paying admission, but they were down on thieves. "Lowest form of humanity," they would say. "Lower than a snake." So I was shocked the day I hitchhiked all the way from Dallas to visit them and found them planning to steal some watermelons from old man Jones's watermelon patch. The boys talked about how good his melons were. Then they told some stories about Jones himself—particularly about his shooting people who got into his patch. But, they said, they thought he didn't guard it much anymore.

When You Make a Bad Choice

Larry, the next to the youngest, was tall and probably the most honest of the group. He kept saying he wouldn't do it and didn't think we should. I agreed, saying that I thought it was wrong to steal watermelons. But Chester egged us on. He said it wasn't really stealing: "A lot of those melons will probably rot in the field, and what are one or two watermelons among so many? If old farmer Jones weren't so stingy, he'd give us some melons."

When it grew dark, four of us, including Nick and I, got into Chester's car. We drove down the dirt road to the Joneses' farm. Satisfied that no one was guarding the patch, we got out of the car. Chester stayed in the car, saying, "If I see someone, I'll honk. Then you guys beat it back to the car."

We crawled carefully through the barbed-wire fence and started thumping watermelons. They were big, ripe, and ready for picking, and we could hardly wait to taste one! Then Chester tooted his horn. We ran toward the car, but Chester took off as fast as he could, leaving us behind. As we were running through the field, we could hear someone shouting at us, and then we heard the sound of a shotgun being fired. I was sure the shot had just missed us. Then I heard a second shot. By this time I was nearly airborne!

When I reached the fence, I didn't crawl through it. Instead, I dived through it head first. However, my aim was bad. The thin khaki pants I had on—the only pair I had brought on the trip—were ripped almost the full length of the pant leg. The barbed wire also scored my leg pretty badly, so it was bleeding.

I lay in the ditch, listening for the shotgun, and making all kinds of promises to the Lord. I knew I'd made a really bad choice. Then I heard laughter! Nick and I had been set up and completely duped. Larry had cleared his plan with "farmer Jones" and then had gone to the field and lain in wait for us. Chester's toot of the car horn had signaled him to begin the "attack." I spent the rest of the weekend in badly torn pants!

I made another bad choice several years later. After Camille and I were married, we returned to college to finish our degrees. We chose to go to Andrews University. We thought this was a logical choice and wondered why everyone at Southwestern, which was a junior college at the time, didn't skip Union and go directly to Andrews, particularly if they were going to the seminary after college. We soon found out why: The academic programs didn't jive. By the time I found this out, they had taken away almost a whole year's credits! To me, it was ridiculous stuff. They hadn't accepted any credits for several subjects I had taken at Southwestern, such as Daniel and the Revelation, which Andrews taught on the "upper biennium," and homiletics, which is a class on preaching. I had to take these two classes and several others over again.

I wanted to graduate in two years, so I began to try to work this out. I'd always gotten along well with my teachers; many of them are among my best friends even today. But occasionally I ran into someone who didn't like me. The registrar at Andrews was one of those people. We spent so much time arguing about subjects that his resentment of me became evident. I'm sure he had his reasons because I wasn't happy with the situation. Frankly, I still think it stinks! I hope our colleges have progressed to the place where they all accept the credits given by one another. After all, they are sister institutions.

I had worked on correspondence courses worth eleven credit hours—which I needed in order to graduate on time—while Camille and I spent the summer on that fire tower in Idaho. However, months went by, and I could never seem to find a convenient opportunity to take the final tests. Eventually, I found someone who would administer the tests for me—a minister who had come back to the seminary for a semester. I sent his name and address to the correspondence school, Home Study Institute, now called Griggs University. They sent the test to him, and he gave the envelope to me and said, "Bring this on Sunday morning, and I'll give you the test."

I don't know whether he noticed, but the envelope containing the two tests wasn't sealed. I resisted the temptation to look at the questions for several days as I studied for these finals. I knew the subjects well. Then about midnight on Saturday night, my curiosity got the best of me and I peeked. Immediately, I was sorry that I had. I'd made a very bad choice! I was ashamed of myself for cheating. And compounding my remorse, I realized I had anticipated all the questions on the test. I hadn't needed to look at the test to ace it!

However, I began to rationalize too. My resentment said, *"You shouldn't have to take this class anyway. It's only because of their dumb system that you have to retake all these subjects. So what if you cheated on the whole thing!"*

I quieted my conscience with that kind of reasoning and decided not to say anything about what I'd done. I took the test, made an "A" grade, graduated, and went into the ministry. Every once in a while, though, I'd think about what I'd done. Sometimes when I was praying, it would come to my mind. *I have to make this right,* I thought. *I need to face the folks at Home Study Institute and tell them what I did.*

One day Camille and I were driving through the Washington, D.C., area. As we drove near the General Conference headquarters, which was located in Takoma Park at that time, I told her about the incident and that I had to make it right. We parked, and I walked into the lobby and asked if I could see Dr. Delmer Holbrook, the president. The secretary assured me that he would be happy to see me. When I turned away from her desk, I found myself face to face with the Andrews registrar, who had just stopped by to see Dr. Holbrook as well. Now, this was a real test! All Dr. Holbrook had to do was to tell the registrar that he should nullify my degree because I had cheated, and he could take care of it almost on the spot! I broke into a sweat.

My name was called, and I went in to see Dr. Holbrook. And then I did one of the most difficult things I have ever done: I confessed my wrongdoing to this man. I told him that I didn't know what this would mean, especially since the registrar was waiting to see him next, but that I had to get this off my conscience.

Dr. Holbrook looked at me and said, "You are forgiven. Don't ever worry about this again. It has taken guts for you to tell me this. As the president of this school, I have the authority to forgive you, and I've just done it." He had prayer with me, shook my hand, and sent me on my way. As I left his office, the registrar gave me one of his stern looks. I smiled at him and even offered my hand to him, and I can't be sure, but I thought I saw a twinkle in his eye!

We've all made some bad choices in life. Sometimes we carry the guilt around for years. It will kill us if we keep carrying it! Finding release is simple. I was ready to offer to do make-up work, outside reading—whatever was necessary to make my cheating right. But Dr. Holbrook said it was within his power to forgive me—and he did.

We have a heavenly Father who has promised to do the very same thing! So don't give up when you do something you shouldn't. Turn to Jesus. The Word says, "If we confess our sins, he is faithful and just to forgive us our sins, and to cleanse us from all unrighteousness" (1 John 1:9, KJV).

Keep on keeping on, even when you've made a bad choice—after you ask forgiveness, that is!

CHAPTER FOUR

WHEN YOU ARE FALSELY ACCUSED

A s a student, like many others, I had to work to pay part of my educational expenses. My dad was not very excited about my going off to a church boarding school. He had his hands full keeping a roof over our heads and food on the table. He was a hard worker, a great father, and a good provider, but he didn't see the need, nor did he have the money, for me to go away to school when there was a school just down the street in Dallas that he paid for with his taxes.

However, Mom felt that a Christian education was a priority, so she rented to an elderly woman the one room in our house that had a private entrance and bath, and she fixed the woman three meals a day. With that room-and-board money, she paid my tuition.

I was responsible for the balance of my school expenses, so I worked at many jobs, none of which paid much money. The summer before my senior year, a friend introduced me to a young man whom I'll call Hans. When I told him about the summer jobs I'd had, he said his employer hired students to fill in for the full-time employees who were taking their vacations. He told me his name and address and said that if I contacted him in the spring, he'd put my name in for summer employment. So, during a weekend leave that spring, I decided to look Hans up. John Lewis, a friend of mine from church, lived only a block from my house. I invited him to go with me.

Hans told us he had some errands to run and said we could talk while riding with him. While he was taking a shower and changing clothes, John showed me a document that was lying out in plain view. It was a certificate of discharge from the state penitentiary in Huntsville, Texas. My gut told me to get out of there, and John felt the same way, but we were in an awkward position. Neither of us wanted to embarrass Hans.

Hans came back into the room while we were looking at the certificate. After we got in the car with him and drove away, he brought up the subject of his criminal record. He told us that he'd spent three years in the penitentiary for writing hot checks. He also said he'd committed seventeen armed robberies that the authorities knew about, but they hadn't had enough evidence to charge him with the crimes.

I noticed a hunting knife in the back seat of the car. It had a long blade, but the point of the blade was broken off. I asked him about the knife, and he said a friend had asked him to take it to work to grind a new point on it, which I assumed was true. Hans then tried to sell us some razor blades. He had a large supply of them in a sack that he said he'd bought at a garage sale earlier that day. But we didn't want to spend what little change we had on razor blades.

Hans picked up a girlfriend and took her to the bus station. She asked him to keep her radio and a police officer's nightstick, or billy club, which a friend who was a cop had given her. After completing this errand and several others, Hans pulled into a twenty-four-hour coffee shop, and we had a bite to eat and talked about summer work. He took our names and phone numbers and very little additional information. *If this is all he needs,* I thought, *we could have given it to him back at his room.* It seemed he just wanted someone to talk to. However, the more he told us about himself and the more we observed, the stronger grew our feeling that we would never see him again after that night.

We got into Hans's car and started to pull away from the restaurant. As we did so, police cars surrounded us and forced us to pull over to the curb. The officers pulled us from the car and frisked us for weapons. The officer who searched me said, "This one's clean."

I cracked back, "Of course, I just showered a few hours ago!"

I quickly learned that these officers had no sense of humor at all. They were on a mission, and they were very serious. Hans was their target. There was no telling what he was guilty of, but John Lewis and I were totally innocent of whatever it was—or so we thought!

In searching the car, the police found the razor blades. They said those razor blades were weapons.

"How are they weapons?" I asked.

They described several ways razor blades can be used as weapons and said that Hans had too many for them to be for shaving purposes. Unfortunate timing on stocking up on razor blades!

They also found the nightstick and informed us this was an illegal weapon. And even without its point, the hunting knife was beyond legal length. So, the police arrested all three of us for carrying concealed weapons. John and I insisted that we were only passengers in Hans's car. But that didn't matter; we were headed for jail.

The police handcuffed us, loaded us into different squad cars, and took us to a substation. They told us that detectives would interview us, and then, if we were charged, we could make bail and be released. One of the officers told me, "I think they'll let you and your buddy go pretty soon."

With that assurance, I called my dad. It was late—well after ten o'clock by now—and every night, Dad went to bed right after the ten o'clock news, so I knew my call would awaken him. But I felt it would be better to let him know what was happening now, rather than later. I assured him I'd be home before very long.

Then I learned we would be taken to the main city jail for our interview with the detectives, there being none at the substation. About an hour later, a paddy wagon picked us up and transported us to the downtown jail—the jail where, later, Jack Ruby gunned down Lee Harvey Oswald. On the way there, the young police officer at the wheel had a great time throwing his handcuffed prisoners, who had nothing to hold on to, all over the back of the paddy wagon. He had also picked up another prisoner, a drunk, at the substation, which made the ride even worse. The louder we yelled for him to slow down and take it easy, the faster and rougher he drove.

At the jail, the officers had each of us put our few possessions into envelopes. Then they fingerprinted us and took our pictures. I've often wished I could see the picture they took of me that night. I'm sure it would be hilarious!

Then, off to the jail cells we went. We were put in a tank, which is a large cell with no chairs or tables and no mattresses or blankets, only hard steel bed frames. Most of the inmates sat on the floor, and a few were standing. Some were drunks trying to sleep off their inebriation. The scents of B.O., cigarette smoke, and Pinesol made a sickening combination I will never forget!

I kept wondering when the detectives would come to talk to us. I asked the jail guard who walked by when I could talk to a detective. He told me that, contrary to what you see on TV, for the most part, detectives don't work at night. They work the day shift.

The guard said the detectives would interview us at about eight or nine, after their morning meeting with their staff. I was aghast! It was two o'clock in the morning by now, and I knew my parents would be worried—or even worse, infuriated! So I talked the guard into letting me use the phone again. When Dad answered, I could tell he was really upset with me. "Jim, tell me the truth. What did you do to get arrested?" he asked.

I assured him I was completely and totally innocent.

"The police don't arrest innocent people," he said in a voice much louder than his usual soft speech.

"That's what I always thought," I said meekly. "Dad, the guy we were with is bad business, but John and I have done nothing."

About six in the morning, they rallied us all for breakfast, the most memorable one of my whole life. It consisted of a cup of coffee, a piece of bread, oatmeal with raisins (to this day I hate raisins in my oatmeal), and half a canned peach. I took one bite of the oatmeal. How bad can you make oatmeal? It was horrible! The peach was all I would eat. So, John and I became very popular. Neither of us wanted our coffee or other food, and the old timers were happy to take it off our hands.

A guard placed a phone with a long cord in the cell, and we lined up to make calls. With this crowd, you waited your turn patiently. Most of the prisoners were calling attorneys.

When it was my turn, I called home. My mother answered the phone. By this time, I was frantic. "Mom, I've got to get out of here," I said. "Please tell Dad to get me a lawyer." I'd seen a number of people leave their cells with attorneys, and I was seeing attorneys in a new light!

"Don't worry," Mom said. "I've called Pastor Leach."

Ben Leach was our pastor, and I had great respect and admiration for him. But he was the last person in the world whom I wanted to know that I was in jail!

"Mom, why did you tell the pastor?" I yelled excitedly into the phone. "I don't want anyone to know I'm in jail, especially the pastor! I don't need a preacher. I need a lawyer."

When I hung up the phone, I was frustrated and discouraged. This was the first time I realized I have a slight case of claustrophobia. I couldn't stand small, confined spaces. I simply had to get out of there!

Meanwhile, a lot of people were working on the outside to get John and me out. My father had called his sister, my aunt Opal. She was the receptionist and phone operator for a large Ford dealer, and she and her boss knew everyone in town. My aunt was especially friendly with the chief of police in neighboring Highland Park. She called him and told him that John and I were active church members and sang in the choir. This was true, but I would hardly have called us choirboys!

John's mother was Pastor Leach's secretary at the church. She had also called Pastor Leach, and he had headed for the jail, where he began working for our release. My dad was doing the same thing in another part of the building.

Finally, a jailer called my name. I jumped up and was escorted into a room where my dad was waiting. I was never so happy to see him in my entire life! That happiness, however, was dampened by the fact that I knew he had five children, including four sons, and the one who just had to go off to a Christian school was the only one he ever had to bail out of jail. I was embarrassed, ashamed, and frustrated with the circumstances that had landed me there.

Dad was very serious as he talked to me. "Jim," he said, "we're going to visit with a detective. [*Finally*, I thought.] You don't say anything but 'Yes, sir' or 'No, sir.' If you shoot off your mouth or sass this officer, not only will you be in big trouble with the law, you will be in even bigger trouble with me."

I'd rather be in trouble with the law than in trouble with my dad, so I held my tongue as the detective read the riot act to me. I felt the police owed me an apology for false arrest, and this detective was telling me all they could do to me and how lucky I was they were letting me go without charging me. Holding my tongue and replying only "Yes, sir" and "No, sir" was very difficult indeed, for I'd spent the whole night thinking of things that I could say! Once, I started to say something in my own defense, and Dad caught my eye. The look he gave me said, "Don't you say a word," and I held my tongue.

Soon it was over. An officer returned my billfold, comb, and change, and I was released. The air outside felt so clean! I was exhausted. I was also starved, so my dad took me to a small café near the station, and I had a late breakfast. I poured out my heart to my dad, telling him how embarrassed I was. I will never forget the reassurance he gave me. He made it very clear to me that in the real world, things like this happen. He told me he still believed in me. However, he also made it clear he had told me for years that I had to be careful whom I associated with. When I realized Hans was a bad person, I should have excused myself and gotten away from him. I knew Dad was right.

Later, Pastor Leach told me, "Jim, you're going to be a preacher some day. You can tell this story, but don't ever tell anybody it happened to you! People get things mixed up. If you tell it about yourself, they'll have you guilty of something."

Well, as you can see, I've ignored his advice. But this is a different age, a "tell-all" time, and this story is quite tame compared to the things people are arrested for today! False accusations bother me far worse than being accused of something of which I *am* guilty! It is often so difficult to prove one's innocence.

Someone may have falsely accused you—the authorities, your wife or husband, your boss, teacher, or someone else. If so, it is a time to pray, to seek the advice of a wise friend or counselor, and to wait on the Lord. It is not a time to panic. Being accused doesn't make you guilty.

Remember the Bible's story of Joseph, the son of Jacob. The wife of Potiphar, his employer, accused him falsely, and he was thrown into jail and left there until the Lord opened the way out. God used this misfortune to bring Joseph to the attention of the pharaoh and, in time, to make Joseph the prime minister of Egypt. Our Lord can take the darkest of all circumstances and turn them into a spotlight of greatness for Him and for you. Jesus said, "Blessed are you when people insult you, persecute you and falsely say all kinds of evil against you because of me. Rejoice and be glad, because great is your reward in heaven" (Matthew 5:11, 12, NIV).

In time, Joseph's name and reputation were cleared. Though some at Potiphar's house may have gone to their graves thinking he was guilty, it was far more important that God knew the truth!

Keep on keeping on, even when you are falsely accused.

CHAPTER FIVE

WHEN YOU'RE HAVING
MARRIAGE DIFFICULTIES

For me, it all started one warm, summer night while I was lying in bed on the screened-in sleeping porch on the side of our house on Belmont Street in Dallas. I was about sixteen at the time.

I remember having some very serious thoughts about the future while I was trying to get to sleep. I began to wonder whom I was going to marry and where she was that night. I did something that is a bit unusual, I think. I prayed for her. I prayed that the Lord would choose the girl I was to marry! Then I began to wonder whether I could really trust Him to do that. I thought of several girls I knew, and I worried, *What if He were to choose one of them? He wouldn't do that to me, would He?*

I was sure, though, that I could trust God and that I would be pleased with His choice if I would just wait on Him and not try to manipulate the decision. So, I prayed that He would protect her, wherever she was—keep her pure. And I vowed to try to stay pure, saving myself for her.

Occasionally, I would think of that night, and I would renew that prayer for her and for God's guidance. I also prayed that the Lord would let me know, in a very definite way, when I met her. I had no idea how He would do that, but I assumed that I would know when it happened.

The last semester of my senior year in academy, I heard there was a new girl on the campus. For several days our paths didn't cross.

Then one day as I was leaving L. C. Evans Hall, the main classroom building, I crossed paths with a girl whom I had never seen before. I held the door open for her and said, "Hello." She answered, and we both continued on our separate ways. I will never forget that I thought at the time, *I wonder if that's the girl the Lord has chosen for me to marry?* In all honesty, I had never wondered that about any other girl before, nor did the thought ever occur to me again.

That doesn't mean Camille and I got together right away. In fact, a friend of mine, Roger Thompson, beat me to her and started asking her to go to school functions with him. Once, Roger, Camille, and I went to Dallas for some type of event and stopped by my house so that I could pick up something. My mother met Camille and fell in love with her immediately. She asked me, "Why don't you go after that Camille? I really like her."

"Well, Mom," I replied, "she's Roger's girlfriend; she's already taken." But I knew if I ever had the opportunity, I would make my move.

That opportunity came in the fall, when Roger decided not to return to school. I asked Camille for a date, and she accepted. When I called for her at the dorm, she looked so great that I was completely overcome by her beauty. As we walked down the steps of the dorm and started up the sidewalk toward the center of the campus, I suddenly stopped and took her into my arms and kissed her right on the lips with a passionate kiss! She was shocked. What kind of nut was this? She quickly let me know this was to stop, at least until a more appropriate time.

I would have asked her to marry me that night because I was so sure she was the one, but I decided she would think that was a bit soon. So, I waited until the one-week anniversary of our first date! Amazingly, she said, "Yes," and we were engaged. That may not have been as crazy as it sounds. I had watched her closely for several months as she dated my friend Roger.

However, Camille broke up with me the next spring. I've told about that experience in greater detail in my first book, *The Battle Is the Lord's.* Let me just say here that I was devastated. My heart was broken. At the suggestion of the college president, I left school for a week rather than quitting altogether. I returned with resolve to keep going, but I was dying inside—often depressed and discouraged, spending a lot of time in prayer. "Lord," I said, "I really thought she was the one. Where did I go wrong?" The next year without Camille was difficult. During that time, I did a lot of growing up.

Almost a year after Camille terminated our engagement, she and I helped the Bible teacher, M. D. Lewis, whom everyone called "Elder," conduct a funeral in a small town away from the campus. I sang, Camille played the piano, and Elder had the sermon. We had talked in the car on the way there and back, and then Elder called his wife, Barbara, to meet us at a Chinese restaurant, where he treated us to a great dinner of egg foo yong, vegetable fried rice, and Chinese vegetables. We had a good time visiting, though I was guarding my emotions. Some of Camille's friends had told me she wanted us to get back together. I wasn't so sure that was true, and I was determined to protect myself from being hurt so deeply again. I had no plans of our getting back together.

Then one night I received a call from, of all people, the girls' dean, Miss West. "I want you to come over to the dorm," she said in a very demanding tone.

"Why?" I asked.

"Because I've got a girl over here who's crying her eyes out," she replied.

I knew she was talking about Camille, but I decided this was the time to play hard to get. I told her I would not be coming to the dorm that night; I had other things to do!

Miss West's tone got even harder, and her voice threatening. "Listen here, young man," she said. "If you don't come over here immediately, you will never be welcome in this dormitory, and you can forget about calling for any of my girls at any time. Do you understand?"

She can't do that, I thought, but I decided not to try her. Perhaps she did have that power! So, I agreed to come. A few minutes later she ushered Camille and me into the "fish bowl"—the mostly glass room in the lobby intended for dating couples, which few people, if any, ever used! As Miss West closed the door, she said, "You two get this thing worked out between you." Somehow we did!

That July, we were married in Houston in the new Central Church that Camille's father, Roy Thurmon, had started building just before he had taken the appointment to Collegedale to be the pastor of the college church. Ours was the first wedding in the church after it was finished. I was nineteen years old. Both of us had finished just two years of college, and I had less than $150, which included a one-hundred-dollar bill that one of my uncles had given me as a wedding gift.

My father let me know that he definitely agreed with my choice of a life's mate but that he thought we should wait until we were older. I didn't tell him we had to hurry up and get married because I was afraid that otherwise, we would break up again! *We're not very good at going together,* I thought. *Sure hope we are better at being married.*

Dad had to give his permission for me to get a marriage license, because at that time men younger than twenty-one couldn't obtain one without a parent's permission. (The legal age for women was eighteen, so Camille had no problem.) When I approached the courthouse window, he refused to sign. "You're too young," he insisted. I didn't know whether he was kidding, or serious, or just testing my will. Dad being Dad, only he truly knew. But from my bombastic response, he knew that *I* was serious, and he begrudgingly signed.

Our wedding was very simple and inexpensive, though well attended by friends, family, and fellow church members. Camille's grandfather, E. H. Sweet, came all the way from Winter Haven, Florida, to walk his oldest granddaughter down the aisle. Her father conducted the wedding. My oldest brother, Ed, who is nearly fourteen years older than I, was my best man. My brothers John and Paul stood with me as well, and Camille's friends were her bridesmaids. Camille's dad had always said he wanted grape juice served at his only daughter's reception because of the grape juice that Jesus had supplied at the wedding in Cana. They brought the Welch's all the way from Tennessee.

When the wedding and reception were over, Camille and I left the church in my car. People followed us in a long stream of cars, honking their horns and driving like nuts. I was determined to lose them, and when the light at an intersection was changing, I hit the accelerator, going through the red light before the traffic waiting for green on either side could move. I lost those who were following us, but the first argument of our marriage began immediately because I had clearly run a red light—though I insisted it was pink.

Our honeymoon consisted of one night in nearby Galveston. "We'll have a honeymoon on our trip to Montana," I assured Camille. We had no money, but we both had the promise of teaching jobs that fall in little public ranch schools near Jordan, Montana.

The Monday after our one-night honeymoon, we traveled back to Dallas, where I continued my summer job, earning the money to pay our way to Montana. We made the trip by way of Tennessee to see Camille's folks and then on to Michigan to scout out Andrews University. We planned to continue the quest for our college degrees there, after teaching long enough to make the money we needed to return to school. From Michigan, we drove west toward Montana. We were both seeing a lot of the country for the first time.

Camille and I weren't quite ready for the reality of eastern Montana. As we drove west out of Miles City toward Cohagen and on to Jordan, the absence of trees was striking. We saw, basically, only one large tree. Near it, someone had put up a sign that said, "Lone Tree National Forest." It was their idea of a joke—a good one, I might add. There was an intersection near that tree. When people were giving directions, they'd say, "Go to 'the tree' and turn right," or whatever. There actually were other trees, small ones, which people had planted around their houses. But there weren't many houses. That area was mostly open range, on which sheep, cattle, deer, and antelope grazed. We stopped and stared for a long time at the first herd of antelope we saw. Though we never tired of seeing them, before long we stopped considering them an oddity.

In Jordan, we met the superintendent of schools for Garfield County, Fern Schillriff, and had our orientation. Fern was a "good ol' gal" who made us feel welcome. Things were so strange to us, no one could have made us feel at home, but welcome was enough. We were assigned to the Hafla and Pitzer schools. These schools were located on a gravel road about twenty-five miles off the paved highway between Miles City and Jordan. Our address was Cohagen.

The town of Cohagen consisted of a very few houses; a gas station that was also a small store; and two bars, one of them in the store and one with a dance hall connected. In addition, there was a small, white, wooden post office with the Stars and Stripes always flying. Population twenty-three, I believe—certainly no more! Miles City, which had a Safeway and was a big city for the area, was nearly a hundred miles away. I'm not sure what its population was then, but today it's only a few more than eight thousand people, and I doubt that it was larger then.

Camille and I had our very first serious disagreement in Miles City. OK, it was a fight—but only with words! Let's face it, the old saying about sticks and stones is wrong. Words do more harm than sticks and stones ever thought about doing.

As I remember it, we were stocking up on groceries in Miles City, using some money Camille's grandfather had given her. (The trip to Montana had consumed every dime of the money I had.) I asked Camille to let me have five dollars to get a haircut. In those days, if you had more than two weeks' growth of hair, you needed a haircut. I was starting a new job, and I wanted to look sharp.

Camille met my request with a question. "Just exactly how much is a haircut?" she asked.

That set me off. I told her to forget it, she could keep her money, and I stormed away, totally teed off. I didn't want to tell her that a haircut cost $2.50 plus a fifty-cent tip and that I wanted the extra two dollars for a snack or something. Of course, she had caught me in my little scheme. I never have been able to fool her, and that still gets under my skin!

I had on boots and a cowboy hat, and I looked pretty rough, my hair being longer than I usually wore it. I walked into a barbershop and explained to the barber that I had a job teaching and would receive my first check soon. I told him I didn't have any money that day, but I would pay him for the haircut the next time I came to town.

"I don't know you, cowboy," the barber said without taking his eyes off the head of the man whose hair he was cutting.

I introduced myself.

He said, "No, you don't understand. I don't know you, and I don't want to know you. Get out of my shop!"

The customers who were waiting snickered, and I was embarrassed. I felt like a panhandler. I was also angry with Camille, the barber, and the whole world!

As I left the barbershop and started down the sidewalk, I met three large young men about my age. I moved to the right to give them room, but they moved to that side to block my way. I went to the left, and they did the same, determined to make me leave the sidewalk. Those poor bullies had bad timing that day! They didn't realize I'd had the third degree. They didn't know I'd just been thrown out of a barbershop and embarrassed as I'd extended the hand of friendship and tried to become a customer—even if it was on credit! They didn't know I was fed up with their fair city and everyone who lived there or anywhere else in their state. I was homesick and feeling very much alone that day. They were in the wrong place at the wrong time and picked on the wrong guy!

As they came toward me, I picked out the one in the center as the leader and hit him as hard as I could. I walked right on by, never slowing my pace. Looking back at them, I found the first respect I'd had since coming to town.

When I left Dallas, my dad owed me some money for some work I had done for him. He didn't have it when I left, but he said, "If you need it later, let me know." I had never really planned to bother him for it, but I was in need. I called my dad, and he wired me fifty dollars. I went to another barbershop and got a haircut. Next, I found Camille, asked her if she needed any money, and if so, just exactly how much. Then we both laughed. We had survived our first fight in Montana. Since then, Camille and I have used the line "Exactly how much is a haircut?" on each other hundreds of times. It's funny now, but it was a very sore spot at the time!

It was while we were in Montana that we decided to have three separate accounts: "hers," "mine," and "ours." That doesn't work for everyone, but it certainly does for us. The "ours" account is the largest and pays the bills. The other two are discretionary funds and allow each of us some financial freedom.

I learned to love the people of Miles City—especially Mr. A. G. Miller, the president of the First National Bank, who loaned us twenty-seven hundred dollars to buy stock in a new company that a friend had told us about. The price of the stock more than tripled, and we sold enough to pay off the loan and used the rest to help with our education. Early in our marriage, we learned that it is important to invest what money you have, but never to invest more than you are willing to lose. Later in life, we would lose as well as gain. When investing, you have to be willing to lose as well as to have success.

The schools where Camille and I taught were located just four miles apart. We lived in the teacherage at her school, which had nine students. I had six students, all with the last name of Hafla. Their fathers were brothers, Joe and Anton. The local people said they needed two schools because the road between them was impassable in the winter. There may have been some truth to that, though I drove that road every single day that school year. We felt the reason there were two schools had more to do with the desire of the families in the area for control than with transportation or the weather.

The teacherage where we lived was a one-room, freestanding structure that measured, on the outside, eleven by thirteen feet. It had no running water and no closet, and the toilet was of the outdoor variety. It was about thirty yards from the house. I can guarantee you that on cold nights, when the temperature was below zero, we didn't linger!

The school committee paid one of the families to provide us with water. They brought a three-gallon can of water five days a week at the beginning of the school day. We needed a little extra when we moved in and went to their house with the empty can. We had to give a dollar to Godfrey, the neighbor, to get the can filled from their well. That might not seem like much money now, but believe you me, it was a lot then. The whole idea of charging the new teachers for a little water seemed something less than hospitable!

Three gallons of water a day for drinking, cooking, bathing, and whatever other needs a person has, isn't much. We would pour the contents of the milk can into a large pail we used for drinking and cooking, and the balance into the old liner of an abandoned hot water heater we used as a holding tank. That water would accumulate until Friday evening, when we would take our weekly bath in a wash-tub. Any other baths were of the washcloth variety.

For our weekly bath, I would bring in the tub. Camille would heat a kettleful of water and pour it into the tub, adding some cold water from our tank. Usually, we had only enough water for one filling, so "ladies first" was the rule. I bathed second, in the used water. I did draw the line on Camille's shaving her legs in the tub, though. That was too much even for me!

Our teacherage had electricity but no television, and the radio reception was weak except for some of the powerful Canadian stations. One of the families did have a television and a very tall antenna. One night they called us. (We did have a telephone. A party line, which included everyone in the neighborhood, had just become available that very year.) "Come over and watch TV," they invited. "It's coming in great!"

We jumped into our car and raced to their home. But we could barely make out the figures, the snow on the TV screen was so bad and the picture so faint. The neighbors kept bragging about the reception, but we couldn't even tell what program they were watching! Eventually, we excused ourselves and went home, disappointed.

Needless to say, we found our entertainment in simple things. Very few cars traveled down the gravel roads in that area. When one passed, there was no stopping our students from running to the window to see who was passing by, and after a few days, we were doing the same! Usually, we would know who was passing by. If we didn't, we could pick up the phone and hear people up and down the line speculating on who it was who drove by in that "city car."

Our neighbor Godfrey became our entertainment. Just observing him was quite amusing, and listening to Anton Hafla tell stories about him was better than watching television. Anton told these stories very animatedly. He would laugh so hard every time he told them that you couldn't help but laugh with him!

Once, Anton said, Godfrey ran outside to see a car that was passing by on the road several hundred feet from his house. He didn't recognize the car, so he began to wave frantically for the people to stop. Thinking perhaps someone was hurt or needed help, the driver stopped the car, turned around, and drove up to Godfrey. As he was rolling down his window to ask what the problem was, Godfrey beat him to the punch. He asked loudly (he didn't hear well and always talked loudly), "What do you want?" Dumbstruck, the travelers just sat there, while Godfrey, his curiosity satisfied, turned and walked into his house!

When Godfrey lost track of things, he often accused his neighbors of stealing them from him. One day he accused Anton of stealing his two milk cows. Anton protested that he hadn't taken Godfrey's cows and that he should look somewhere else for them. Godfrey looked everywhere. Then one day he noticed a peculiar smell coming from his silo. He hadn't gone there recently because it contained only the feed for his milk cows, and they were missing so he hadn't needed the feed. When he opened the silo door, he found his two milk cows. They had wandered in and been trapped when Godfrey, not knowing they were there, had closed the door. The cows had literally eaten themselves to death, becoming so full of grain that they bloated, which killed them.

Godfrey had a very ugly dog. This dog would run behind his pickup everywhere Godfrey drove. Most dogs like to ride in pickups, and I asked Anton why Godfrey's dog never rode with him. "Oh, he used to," Anton said. "Then one day Godfrey was driving across the dam of his pond with his dog in the pickup cab. Noticing a car driving down the road, he hung his head out the window of his pickup, trying to see who was passing by. He lost control of the pickup and turned it upside down in the pond. Both Godfrey and the dog escaped, but the dog would never ride with him again!"

The rest of the family was not so fortunate—they still had to ride with him. One night Godfrey was returning from Miles City with his wife. At that time there was open range in that part of Montana. The cows were branded and roamed freely until roundup, when the ranchers would trade back strays that had their neighbors' brands.

Now, very few people drove slower than eighty miles per hour on those gravel roads in Montana, and some drove even faster. Godfrey drove fast and thought slow! Nearing their ranch, that night, he sped over a hill—and right into a herd of cows that was occupying the road. There was a terrible collision. Not only did it kill several of the cows, but it also destroyed his car. Luckily, neither Godfrey nor his wife was injured.

Godfrey came out of the wreckage sputtering, "I'll sue whoever owns these cows. I'll sue them. I'll sue them." But his wife stopped him in his tracks. "Godfrey," she said, "that looks like our brand." It was! Godfrey had run into his own cattle. Not only did he lose the cattle, he had no recourse against anyone else. The entire loss was his. Only Godfrey!

However, life in Montana wasn't all Godfrey stories and fun for Camille and me. We had a lot of adjusting to do with each other. Both of us are strongly opinionated people. Camille's family, especially her brother James, would tease me by saying that Camille would lead me around by the nose. They knew she was strong. When I was with them, I learned not to express my ideas too vigorously so that Camille and I would get along. I sometimes felt that she took advantage of me when we were with her family. However, our roles reversed around my family. They would think, "Poor Camille! Jim is so bossy; she has to put up with a lot."

When I tell about our romance and breaking up and how it broke my heart, people will sometimes come up to Camille and say, "How could you have been so mean to him?"—which, of course, is exactly what I want them to think and to say! The truth is that I deserved it. I was too controlling. I wanted to tell her what to wear and what to eat and to dictate every minute of her life. Of course, she was also trying to change me. I have always loved her, and I believe she loved me too, but there have been challenges through the years. Because both of us were strong-willed and wanted our own way, our relationship was often rocky.

I encourage all couples to keep working on their marriage. This relationship is like a great machine: It needs constant tweaking and updates. You have to put a lot into it to make it worthwhile. That is still true today for us, more than forty-four years after our wedding day. We have learned to disagree without being terribly disagreeable.

We both credit Bill Gothard's Basic Youth Conflicts seminar with helping us to achieve greater harmony in our home.

Montana was like a boot camp for our marriage. We had contracted to teach school for 180 full days, and we knew we couldn't afford to make any trips home until that school year was over. So, we were confined in that small room without having close friends or family near to whom we could complain about each other. We had no place to which we could escape when we had disagreements, and there were more than a few!

When we had completed our 180 days of teaching, we headed first to Texas and then on to Tennessee. We saw some of our friends, and they told us about some couples who were married the very same summer we were and had already divorced.

"Why?" we asked.

"Oh," they said, "she called him a bad name, and he left."

We looked at each other and laughed out loud. "You've got to be kidding!" we said. "They split over something like that? They should have been in Montana!"

We were glad the Lord brought us together and gave us a difficult place in which to begin our marriage. Everywhere we lived after that start was an improvement. The difficulties we faced had been a blessing; they'd made us grow.

I don't want to overemphasize the problems Camille and I have had in our marriage. We have a great relationship. However, I think it is wrong for ministers to portray their marriages as perfect. I remember an evangelist who had a sermon titled, "The Secret of a Happy Home." Everyone who knew his marriage knew that he was speaking from theory. His advertising would have been more truthful if he had used a title like "How to Survive a Difficult Marriage" or "How to Survive a Marriage Crisis."

I've known only one couple who never had a marriage disagreement: Gene and Lucy Fletcher. Camille and I worked with them in evangelism for ten years. A few years after we started working together, they told me that they had never had a single disagreement. I believed them, because I have never seen any couple so completely devoted to each other and in such agreement. They asked me not to say anything to anyone about it, and I didn't—until the next time I preached on marriage. I told the congregation about Gene and Lucy and continued doing so for several years. Their story was just too good to keep to myself!

One day, Gene came to me and said, "Don't ever tell that story to any congregation again."

"Why?" I asked. We were doing four or five series of evangelistic meetings each year, and I had been telling their story during each series.

"Because," Gene said, "today, after you told our story, we almost had our first disagreement."

"About what?" I asked with glee.

He said, "I wanted to sing 'Bless This House' for the appeal song, and she wanted to us to do 'Happy the Home,' and we almost had words!"

I laughed so hard! Instead of honoring his request, I added the "almost fight" incident into my story of how they had never had a disagreement.

While giving the final touches to this chapter, I received word that Gene lost his long and courageous battle with Lou Gehrig's disease. Death has once again brought an end, for the time being, to a great marriage. Loyal Lucy stood by his side "in sickness and in health." Now she, with their sons, Larry and Leonard, and a host of friends, look forward to the great resurrection, when they will be reunited for eternity!

You've heard the saying, "When the going gets tough, the tough get going!" There's a bumper sticker that says, "When the going gets tough, the tough go shopping!" The truth is that when the going gets tough, the tough should go to Jesus. Hold on to Him, trust in Him, and never let Him go!

Keep on keeping on even when you're having marriage difficulties. With Jesus, you can make it together!

CHAPTER SIX

WHEN IT ALL GOES UP IN SMOKE

During one of my first days of eleventh grade at the academy in Keene, Texas, I was jarred from my daydreaming by the wailing of a fire siren. Then two older students jumped from their seats and started for the door. Always ready for an opportunity to skip class, I followed close on their heels. One of them asked, "Are you on the fire department?"

I replied, "Yes, I just joined."

No one stopped or questioned me when I climbed on the back of the truck, so I became a member of the Johnson County Fire Department several years before I was old enough to join legally. In fact, as soon as I learned the ropes, I became the "first-in guy"—the person who grabbed a small hose and ran into the burning building, looking for the "hot spot" in order to put out the fire while it was still relatively small. This was considered one of the more dangerous assignments, which the older, wiser men were more than willing to pass on to the young and reckless. "We have wives and kids," they would tell me. "You don't have anything to lose!" And, of course, except for my life, they were right.

I've endured some terrifying experiences while fighting fires. We didn't have proper smoke masks in those days, and the old military canister gas masks just got in the way, so we rarely used them. I remember being on the floor of burning houses, dousing the fire with a large hose, and placing my nose as close to the water as possible to pick up oxygen. Still, I was often overcome by smoke, after which my lungs would hurt for days from smoke inhalation. In those days, the smoke was not nearly as toxic as it is now (due to the synthetic materials used in fabrics and construction materials today). Still, it could kill!

Jere Putnam was one of the firetruck drivers. I always liked to ride with Jere because he could get the top speed from any vehicle he drove. One Saturday night, the alarm went off, and I knew I would never make it to the station in time to catch the truck. So I ran to the Mizpah gate, knowing I could jump on the back of the truck when it slowed to make the turn. Jere was moving pretty fast, so I really had to run hard to catch the truck, but I made it. I was surprised to find I was the only firefighter on the truck other than Jere. I wasn't worried about being the only firefighter on the truck because I knew that other firefighters would be following the truck in their cars, and there would be plenty of us at the fire.

Jere turned the truck toward Alvarado, and a few miles down the highway, he turned onto a dirt road. The dust was terrible, and I was very thankful we were the lead vehicle, because everyone else was eating our dust! We came to a small wooden bridge, which we crossed at full speed. When we were halfway across, the end of the bridge behind us gave way under the weight of the truck. The end in front of us held, which created a ramp effect. The back part of the truck, with me hanging on for dear life, fell toward the creek. Fortunately, we had so much momentum that the truck careened up the ramp and kept right on going! Jere was a great driver and never lost control.

The bump threw me, feet first, high in the air, but I clung to the bar on the back like a trapeze artist. When I came down, I was slammed against the truck. Fortunately, I escaped the incident with only a bloody nose and lip and a few minor bruises. The firefighters behind us saw what happened. They had to turn around and find another way to the fire, so Jere and I had to fight the fire by ourselves for a while.

My background in the fire department led to Camille and I signing up to work with the U.S. Forest Service the second summer after we married. At fire school, we were told that the top graduates would be hired as fire-spotters, while those who didn't do so well would end up working on fire crews. In other words, if we didn't do well, I would be out fighting fires and working trails and Camille wouldn't have a job. And we would have very little time together. In addition, we needed a place where I could finish the eight hours of correspondence courses I needed to complete my college degree. A fire tower would be the perfect place for us.

Needless to say, we were highly motivated. We finished first and second out of a class of about fifty. I won't tell you who was first!

Our high finish earned us our pick of the towers in the Nez Perce National Forest, which was headquartered in Elk City, Idaho. We chose the Sourdough Mountain lookout. We wanted Sourdough in part because the "tower" was a cupola above the cabin where we were to live. The cabin was completely encased by glass windows three or four feet above the floor, 360 degrees. A rough, wooden ladder led to the cupola above, which not only provided a better view but also housed the "fire finder," a piece of equipment marked like a compass that helped pinpoint the exact location of a fire. If a fire broke out close to our cabin, we were expected to fight it ourselves. For fires beyond our reach, we used the fire finder to help headquarters pin down the location and give directions to the firefighters.

The fire tower was up the mountain over twenty miles of the worst excuse for a road you can imagine. The fire control officer and a team drove ahead of us in a four-wheel-drive truck and cut trees that blocked the road. We struggled to follow in our VW bug, which was never quite the same after the trip—probably because we treated it like a jeep!

Life on the fire tower was great. We didn't fully appreciate it then, but oh, would we enjoy the solitude now! How I would love to be writing this chapter on Sourdough Mountain instead of in this cramped plane seat with a coughing passenger across the aisle. Of course, life on the fire tower did have its drawbacks. There was no running water. Our water source was a spring about a mile away. A footpath provided our only access to the spring, so we had to carry the water home by backpack. Lugging the water was one of my duties. Also, our cabin had no electricity. So, at night, we lit a kerosene lamp for light. We used an old wood stove for heating and cooking. And our toilet was the outdoor variety.

The fire control officer supplied us with sourdough starter from a source that had been "alive" for nearly a hundred years—or so he said. We were careful to "feed" some flour to our starter every night and to keep it in a warm, dark place so it could "grow." Camille made some of the best sourdough pancakes and biscuits you can imagine on that old wood stove. She fried the pancakes in a pan on top, and baked the biscuits in the stove's little oven.

Wildlife surrounded us. Every morning we would wake up and carefully peep out the windows to watch the deer and elk that would regularly graze on the tender grass near our cabin. At the first sounds from inside, they would bolt into the forest, so we would be as quiet as possible. For a while, we also enjoyed watching a badger that lived in a nearby den. One day, he challenged Camille as she was returning from the outhouse, and that ended our friendship with him. A large moose loped by our cabin one afternoon as we were sitting on the steps. He never slowed his pace or even looked our way. Obviously, we made no impression on him, but he'll stay in our memory.

Usually, Sourdough Mountain was peaceful and quiet. Still, we were constantly watching for "smokes" rising from the nearby mountains and valleys. Before working for the Forest Service, we'd had no idea that lightning strikes ignite more than 90 percent of forest fires. The Smokey Bear campaign has very effectively reduced human carelessness.

There are few things more awesome and terrifying than watching a lightning storm from a fire tower. The fire towers are located at the tops of mountains, so you are smack in the middle of the storm. Some of the lightning is actually striking around you, and the room is so charged with electricity that you dare not touch anything metal unless it's insulated. For instance, our fire finder was metal. When I did a reading on a lightning strike, I would move the pointer with the eraser of a pencil. I called out the location of the strikes to Camille, and she wrote them down so that we could chart them on a map later. All the while, lightning was literally dancing around us.

After a lightning storm, we'd watch the strike locations for the next few days. If we saw smoke—often just a puff—we would notify headquarters, giving them the location. They would send a plane to fly over the site. If they found the smoldering tree, they would drop a roll of marker paper as close to it as possible. Then a fire team would go to the site and literally cut the fire out of the tree with an axe. If the tree were allowed to smolder too long, it would explode, sparking a forest fire. Since time was of the essence, accurately marking the location of strikes was very important. We had many strikes in our area. One site puffed smoke that was large enough for us to see. We called the firefighters in, and they extinguished it. Fortunately, we had no serious fires in our watch area that summer.

While we lived in the fire tower that summer, a two-way radio provided our only contact with the outside world. We used it sparingly because it depended entirely on batteries, which had to last until the next load of supplies that we received. We would call in our order for groceries and supplies, and the next time a crew was in our area they would deliver the order. Listening to the chatter on the radio didn't use much battery power, but talking did, so we usually just listened for any mention of our lookout, "Sourdough."

One morning as we were going about our activities, we heard an excited voice on the radio. We knew immediately there had been an accident. A tall young man who had gone through fire school with us only a few weeks before had been hit by the rotor of a helicopter. He had suffered a severe head injury but was still alive. The helicopter had landed on uneven terrain. The pilot told the passengers to crouch low until they had moved far enough away from the helicopter to clear the rotary blades. The young man stood up before he was clear, and the blade clipped him.

The injured man was loaded onto the helicopter, which headed for Grangeville, Idaho, where he would be transferred to a plane. We listened and prayed as the pilot gave continuous reports on his condition. He was still alive when they reached the airport and transferred him in to a forest service plane for the trip to Seattle, where he would receive critical medical attention. We could hear headquarters talking with someone on the plane every few minutes. Then we heard the message, "We're turning back." We knew what that meant. The young man's father also worked for the forest service, and we knew he was somewhere in the forest, listening to a radio just as we were. Our hearts ached for him.

Through the years, Camille and I have been in a position to help with other fires. In the late nineties, we were driving from the conference office in Shreveport toward Hope, Arkansas, when we both saw a well house on fire near a nice brick home. I figured the people in the house knew about it so I didn't plan to stop, but Camille said, "I believe the house is on fire too!" That got me to turn around. Inside the house, we found an elderly lady who was unaware of the fire. We called the firetrucks, helped her out of the house, and stayed with her until the firetrucks and her daughter arrived. There have also been several other instances involving a fire in which we have helped.

So, I respect fire, but I don't fear it. However, despite all the experiences I've had, I wasn't prepared for January 5, 2001. The night before, we had attended a meeting at the Alexandria, Louisiana, Adventist church. We were introducing to the members a man whom we were considering hiring to be their pastor. The members had an excellent spirit, so the meeting had gone well. But I've learned not to rush meetings of this nature; all those in attendance must have ample opportunity to have their questions answered. Following the meeting, I had several smaller meetings with leaders of the church who had questions about other issues, and then I met with the prospective pastor (who eventually accepted the call). So, I didn't get home and into bed until nearly three in the morning. Just before I drifted off, I told Camille that I wanted to sleep a little late in the morning. I was grateful that it was Friday and the office was closed that day.

I was awakened early the next morning by the sound of Camille calling my name at the top of her voice. I bounded from the bed and ran to the kitchen, where she pointed to the roof of the townhouse adjoining ours. "Sid's house is on fire!" she exclaimed.

"That's not smoke," I said calmly. "That's steam."

"It's smoke!" she yelled. "Don't you hear the smoke alarm?"

When I removed the earplugs that I wear when I sleep, I could hear the alarm clearly. "Call the fire department!" I yelled.

By this time, Camille was beating on Sid's front door, which was adjacent to ours. I ran around to his garage, which I found half open. Entering, I found his kitchen door unlocked, so I went in to find our neighbor standing dazed and only partially clothed in the kitchen. I grabbed him and forced him to leave the house. He was thoroughly confused and reluctantly followed as I led him to a chair in our living room and covered him with a blanket that Camille supplied.

In just minutes, the fire department arrived. The firefighters soon extinguished the fire in Sid's downstairs bedroom. They threw his mattress, box springs, and bedding onto the grass a safe distance from the house. Emergency technicians treated Sid on the scene, and then drove him to the hospital in an ambulance, along with his wife, who had come home when she heard about the fire.

Soon the firefighters and investigators left. I was wide-awake, but still dressed in my pajamas with a pair of blue jeans slipped over them. I began to make, receive, and return phone calls. About an hour later, as I was wrapping up a phone call from Jerry Mayes, our Springdale, Arkansas pastor, I saw angry flames shoot across the deck of our townhouse. At the same time, someone began ringing the doorbell and banging on our door. It was another neighbor, Rita Hunt. She was yelling, "Sid's house is on fire again!"

How can this be? I thought. It was obvious that now, the fire was much bigger than it had been before. The alarm and electricity had been cut off during the first fire, and the fire department had not left the customary "watch team." Consequently, the fire had reignited and was now burning unabated. Once again we called the fire department.

Soon I was worried not only about Sid's house but also about ours. Some nearby construction workers rushed into our house and started carrying things out. We backed our cars out of the garage and moved them. I ran to the deck, turned on a garden hose, and began trying to stop the fire from igniting our wooden deck; it was the place where the fire was most likely to spread to our house.

By this time, the firefighters had arrived. They started fighting the fire at Sid's place, even though his house was pretty much a lost cause. I shouted for their help to keep the fire from spreading, but finally gave up in desperation as the flames shot over my head. An old fireman feels pretty bad when he has to stand by and watch his house burn to the ground while believing that it could have been saved with no more than minor damage.

Hours later, when the fire was finally over, we were allowed to walk through the charred debris and look for anything we could salvage. We found practically nothing on the first level. The basement level had suffered extensive smoke and water damage, but we were able to salvage a few things. Camille found some summer clothes, which she immediately took to the cleaners. I had grabbed a few of my clothes from upstairs and had thrown them in the car when the fire first started. That was pretty much all I had salvaged. I had to buy a white shirt and tie to have something to wear while preaching in nearby Minden the next day. Camille had to buy a dress, because the only clothes she had were the ones from downstairs, which were still at the cleaners.

The King of Care, Don Schneider, took time from his unbelievably busy schedule as president of the North American Division of the denomination to call us that night to give encouragement. That meant so much. Over the weekend, when we were in shock, our friends Max and Betty Trevino drove over from Burleson, Texas, to comfort us. It really means the world to have friends who care! Don Hevener drove down from Gentry with his pickup to help clean up the mess and to salvage a few things. Vern Carner called from San Diego and offered to come with his pickup and trailer to help. I assured him we had more help than we could handle—our neighbor Ben Vaughn and his crew and Art Nelson with the conference office workers and their spouses were pitching in. Even though our insurance company promised that we were in "good hands," with a fire like this, one never actually comes out on top financially (or any other way, for that matter). So, the love and even financial help that people poured out in the next month encouraged us greatly.

A few days later after the fire, Camille went back to the cleaners to pick up our clothes. The clerk said, "Oh, Mrs. Gilley! I was so much dreading your coming back, because I have to tell you that our plant across town where we do all of our cleaning burned, and your clothes were burned up with all of the others."

As Camille told me about this on the phone, she burst into tears. It seemed that nothing good was happening to us in January 2001. I assured her that someday we would laugh about this latest catastrophe. It took a while, but I was right. Every time I tell that story, everyone erupts with laughter—not because it's particularly funny, but because it's so ironic!

I'm still looking for some things I fear were lost in the fire. I haven't found the only photo of my father with his great-grandmother, who was nearly a hundred when it was taken. From time to time, other missing items come to mind. Not valuable things, but those personal mementos that I can never replace.

If my experiences with fire taught me anything, it's that we mustn't let our possessions possess us. We must hold what we have loosely! People and truth are important. Guard both with your life. But don't waste any time guarding and worrying about your possessions.

A few weeks after the fire, our friend Sam Green gave us a gray elephant with a card attached that says it was made from compressed ashes from Mount St. Helens. He also gave us a beautiful letter in which he said beauty can come from ashes. It can. So, when your dreams go up in smoke, turn them over to God. Don't waste the experience. Let it draw you closer to Jesus Christ. Our characters are being formed by the combination of our relationship with Him and with our experiences in life. I don't expect you to desire an experience like a house fire, but if one comes your way, don't miss the blessing that can come from that painful experience.

My friend E. E. Cleveland, who knows a lot about suffering, said to me a long time ago, "Gilley, the Lord must be toughening you up for something great someday." I think I know what it is. It's heaven. Jesus knows I have a tendency to depend upon myself, and if I do, I'll be lost. But if I depend upon Him, I'll be saved. The same goes for you.

So, keep on keeping on in your effort to depend upon Jesus even when you hear the sirens of fire engines nearing your house!

CHAPTER SEVEN

WHEN YOU ARE
UNDER ATTACK

The summer of 1966 was a pivotal time in my life. I was finishing my degree at Andrews University, having spent the year before pastoring a small district of three churches: Plainville, Meriden, and Middletown, Connecticut. Camille and our one-year-old son, Jimmy, were spending the summer with Camille's folks in Collegedale, Tennessee, where her dad, Roy Thurmon, was pastor of the college church. I made the trip to visit them as often as possible.

That year, a General Conference session was being conducted in Detroit, and I was planning to spend at least a few hours there on the weekend. It was the first General Conference session I attended. A few days before I was to go, I ran into my friend Don Jacobsen. He asked me if I had heard the news. I didn't know what he was talking about, so he filled me in. Don had attended one of the ministerial pre-sessions and had seen my conference president, Merle Mills. He told Don that the conference committee had voted to make me, an intern with only two years of field experience, the conference evangelist.

I was elated! I loved all aspects of ministry, but evangelism was by far my favorite. I'd had a prayer goal of getting into full-time evangelistic ministry by the time I was twenty-five. It had seemed impossible, and now I was being appointed to that position at the age of twenty-five—the youngest full-time evangelist in North America at that time.

I knew that Pastor Mills had been trying to find an evangelist for several years. None of the established evangelists would consider working full time in difficult New England. Fordyce Detamore, the best of them all, had bombed in Boston, and no one in their right mind would try to do evangelism where Detamore had failed to have his usual success.

Pastor Mills had looked everywhere and could find no one interested. So he called H. M. S. Richards, Jr., and asked him if he knew anyone whom he could get. Richards said, "Why don't you ask Jim Gilley? He's already in your conference, he's held a couple of reasonably successful meetings as a pastor, he worked hard for me when I held the Fitchburg meetings, and he understands the basic mechanics of soul winning and public evangelism." Richards also told Pastor Mills that he had never worked with anyone who had more desire to hold meetings than I did, and he was sure that other conferences were interested in my becoming an evangelist for them.

So, Pastor Mills had taken my name to the conference committee, and they had voted to invite me to take that position. In choosing me, they chose the right man. I was so dumb that I didn't know evangelism didn't work in New England. And I was so anxious to do evangelism that there was no question but that I'd say yes!

That week, Robert Pierson was elected the General Conference president. And then the General Conference committee chose my conference president, Merle Mills, to replace Pierson as president of the Trans-Africa Division. I wasn't sure how that would affect the decision to make me the evangelist.

The circumstances that had led me to the Southern New England Conference in the first place were a bit strange. Unlike most students from Southwestern Junior College, Camille and I hadn't gone to Union College to finish our undergraduate degrees. Instead, we had taken a year off from our studies to work, teaching school in Montana to get enough money to continue our education. Then we went to Andrews to complete our degrees.

In my senior year, a new student came to Andrews from New England. His name was Merlin Mills. He was a brash and opinionated young man who was very athletic. We both were active in the intra-mural sports program, especially flag football and baseball.

I heard that Merlin had said he thought the ministerial students at Andrews were a bunch of pansies, sissies. The next time I played against him, I lined up across from him and blocked him as hard as I could. We were both thin, but I was taller and a little stronger, so I got the upper hand and put him on the ground several times during the game, each time saying, "You ministerial students are a bunch of pansies." Naturally, he was infuriated!

Later that week he walked up to me in a hallway and said, "I understand you are one of those ministerial students too."

I answered, "Yes, and we're not all pansies," at which he laughed—and at that moment, a friendship was born.

One day some time later, Merlin said to me, "Do you know that my father is a conference president?"

I said, "No. I figured your dad must be an infidel." (We frequently teased each other and used "put-down humor.")

"Well," he said, "he is a conference president. I haven't told that to people out here—not because I'm not proud of him; I'm very proud of him. But being the son of a conference president in a little town like South Lancaster has been difficult. That's why I came here in-stead of going to Atlantic Union College, which is across the street from my house."

Merlin went on to tell me that his father was coming out to inter-view some ministerial students and had asked him to line up several for interviews.

"I'm not the least bit interested in going to New England," I told him.

He told me that I didn't have to accept a call, but asked that I do an interview as a favor to him. I told him it was a waste of everyone's time, but that, as a favor to him, I would do it, for by this time we had become very good friends.

For years the Texas Conference president, Ben Leach, had told me he wanted me to come back to Texas. I had a file folder full of his letters of encouragement. However, due to a mix-up concerning which year I was graduating, Pastor Leach had already hired all the interns for which he had budgets. He told me that if I would wait a year, he would have a place for me, but he had none at the time.

The Michigan Conference president, N. C. Wilson, the father of the Neal Wilson who was to serve as General Conference president for so many years, was a prince of a man whom I liked the moment I met him. He also interviewed me and offered me a position, subject to the vote of his conference committee. He told me it would not be official until I received a letter from him. I wanted to work with him and was hoping that his letter would come soon.

Then I met Pastor Mills. I was also very impressed with him. He wouldn't interview me unless Camille was present too. He said that he always interviewed the ministerial students' wives as well and that they played a big role in his decisions. Over the years, I recognized the wisdom of his philosophy. When I became a conference president, I followed his example on this.

In our prayers, Camille and I had told God that we would accept whichever official "call" we received first. A few days after our interview with Pastor Mills, he sent us a letter inviting me to join the staff of the Southern New England Conference as the associate pastor of the South Lancaster Village church, assisting Pastor Russell Adams. We accepted.

A couple weeks after Camille and I arrived in South Lancaster, Merlin Mills was headed back to Andrews for the fall semester. He was riding in a car with his mother and a friend, who was driving. They were involved in a tragic accident, and Merlin was killed—the only one in the car who was seriously injured. So, the first funeral that I had a part in as a minister was Merlin's, the person who was largely responsible for my being in that conference. What a tragic loss to his family and friends and to the ministry! Merlin would have been a fantastic worker for God.

All this brings us back to our story. Three years after I started working in the Southern New England Conference, Merlin's father had named me conference evangelist. Then he had taken a call to Africa as a division president.

I wondered if the person who was elected president in place of Pastor Mills would honor my appointment as evangelist. Pastor Lowell Bock took that position, and he was always supportive.

However, the treasurer, with whom I got along fine on a personal basis, was to present a challenge to me professionally. Shortly after becoming the evangelist, I asked the conference to hire a singer to assist with my meetings. I was told that there was no budget for a full evangelistic team—that I would have to work alone or raise the money for a singer.

I had met David Peterson and really enjoyed his singing. He sounded very much like George Beverly Shea, who sang for Billy Graham. David was building cars for General Motors in Michigan but dreamed of singing full time. I got the head elder of one of the churches in Connecticut I had pastored to give the money to the conference to pay David's salary. However, I wasn't experienced enough to handle the transaction properly. So when my friend gave the money, the treasurer told him the conference needed the money to cover my salary and that I didn't need a singer. My friend was easily intimidated by people like the treasurer, and he let the money be used for that purpose.

So, I had to tell David that I couldn't pay him. But he had already quit his job and was on his way to New England with his wife and four children and their household goods. Some truly difficult days lay ahead for all of us.

That experience with the treasurer floored me, and before I could get up off the floor, I was hit again. A Bible teacher at the college, while teaching a Sabbath School general lesson study to hundreds of students and members of the college church, made fun of the "white-coat evangelist who's running around the conference."

I saw him the next day and asked him to let up on me, as I was having a difficult time getting started. He let me know he certainly wasn't going to let up and kept insisting that I go to an empty room where he could talk to me privately. I genuinely had to hurry on to an appointment and declined his invitation, but I did say that if he per-sisted in opposing evangelism, I wouldn't be able to recommend his department to any prospective ministerial students. This upset him, and I left him in a rage.

A few days later, Lowell Bock, the conference president, called me and told me I would have to come to the office and visit with him, the Bible teacher, and the president of the college. When we met, they presented a long list of charges against me—thirteen or fourteen items. The general idea was that the day of public evangelism was over, that I knew it, and that I was dishonest for not acknowledging it. They also said they had the academic freedom to question the use of public evangelism, but that I didn't have the right to criticize them for their statements.

The college president looked at me and said, "Jim, be honest, you know evangelism in America is dead and no longer effective."

I said, "No sir, I don't know that. But if I were you and I did know that, I would never say it to a young minister who's preaching his heart out."

Pastor Bock asked me to respond to the charges. I had made no notes, but I remembered them by number, an old memory trick from college days, and decided not to take them in order, but started with the tenth charge. I then went to the first charge and went back and forth until I had answered each one, not necessarily to their satisfaction, but giving my view.

When the meeting was over, Pastor Bock asked me to stay for a private meeting with him. He told me he was very proud of how I handled myself, and then he gave me some very good advice. He advised me to mend fences and to be careful not to respond to opposition in such a way as to cause even a good man, like the Bible teacher, to lose his cool. It was good counsel, and I took it.

The conference treasurer was still upset because I had tried to raise the money for a singer and had also purchased six hundred dollars' worth of sound equipment without prior committee approval. He knew that David and his family had moved to South Lancaster, that David had gotten a job, that I was planning on his singing for me at nights and on weekends when our meetings were close by, and that I intended to give him mileage for traveling back and forth to the meetings. The treasurer saw this as an end run around his veto, so, at a meeting of the conference committee, he moved that they fire me for insubordination.

The union conference president, Pastor F. R. Millard, came to my defense, saying he thought I had shown a lot of initiative. He said that I needed guidance and direction, but in his opinion, I had done nothing that would call for such a drastic action.

He was right! I needed a lot of guidance, but I'm glad he didn't let them write me off.

Though I successfully defended myself against these attacks, they were doing great damage to my soul and setting me up for Satan's attacks. I couldn't sleep at night, and I was depressed and very unhappy. The public evangelism that I had dreamed of doing and thought would provide me the most enjoyable time of my life was starting out as an unbelievable nightmare. You've heard of "walking pneumonia." Well, I truly believe that I was having a "walking nervous breakdown."

During that time I made some very poor decisions that were to cost me dearly in years to come. I wish that I hadn't made any major decisions when I was under such stress. I wish that I had gone into a protective mode of operation instead of being ready to act and react so quickly. I wish that I had been wise enough then to practice the "cover up" when in that time of attack.

What is the "cover up"? I'm so glad you asked! It is a strategy that has kept me from overreacting to stressful situations. I've learned over the years to use this strategy, and I'm happy to share it with you and hope that it works for you as it has for me.

When I was a teenager, my good friend Nick Turman's older brother, Buddy, was a world-class heavyweight boxer. He was ranked in the top ten boxers in the world. Nick and I spent a lot of time around the boxing gym watching him train, sparring some ourselves, and talking to fighters and trainers, some of whom were veterans of hundreds of fights and had the scars, cauliflower ears, and strange speech to show for it!

Boxers learn to cover up when they get in trouble in the ring and their opponent is landing a flurry of punches. They do this by holding their boxing gloves in front of their face and holding their arms close together to protect their jaw. This position leaves a relatively small target for their opponent, who usually ends up bouncing punches off the boxer's arms, gloves, and, perhaps, his hard head, where he can take a lot of punching without suffering much damage.

Boxers assume this position until the opponent either "punches himself out"—which means he becomes arm-weary and tired of pounding the boxer—or the boxer regains his strength, or the bell rings, ending the round and allowing the boxer to return to his corner to recover and prepare for another round. If a boxer doesn't assume the cover up and tries instead to trade blows with his opponent when a flurry of punches comes, he often makes a tactical mistake that causes him to get knocked out and lose the fight altogether.

I'm not defending boxing here. Through the years I've come to deplore that "sport." But remember, the apostle Paul used the illustration of the boxer to make a point. That's merely what I'm trying to do!

Here's the point: When you are attacked, go into the cover up! Spend more time with the Lord, on your knees, and in His Word. Make sure you are "covered" by the precious blood of Jesus. Spend more time with good Christian friends. (Everyone needs at least one.) Spend as little time as possible with the person or group who is attacking you. Pray for your enemy, and ask the Lord to help you truly love the person or group who is causing you pain.

And don't make major decisions! Not during this time. Wait until the flurry has ended, one way or the other. Relief will come. The bell will ring!

How I wish that I had known this strategy at that time. Problems don't come one at a time so that you can handle them. They gang up like a pack of dogs and hit you all at once. During this time, Camille was in the final few weeks of pregnancy. In the preceding seven years, she had suffered five miscarriages, one of which had been a beautiful little boy, born premature, whom we had laid to rest in the South Lancaster Cemetery. She had been fighting problems the entire time of this pregnancy, and this brought strain to both of us, severely testing our relationship.

In addition, one of my best friends, a young pastor who was older than I, already ordained, and really more deserving than I, was angry at the conference and me because he hadn't been chosen for the position I had received. He really should have been the logical choice, but no one had the slightest idea he wanted to be the evangelist until

I had been asked. He was bitter and took a call away from the conference. We all missed him. I felt terrible about the loss of this friend, and so did about half the ministers in the conference, many of whom blamed me for his leaving and vowed I would never receive an invitation to hold meetings in their churches.

Because of this problem and my youth, the pastors of the larger churches were not inviting me to hold meetings. So my next series of meetings was in Quinebaug, Connecticut, with Pastor Russell Burrill and his wife, Cindy. How I prayed that the Lord would do something special, for I was so discouraged. That little church had only about thirty members, but they worked hard and so did the pastor. With God's help, we had a great harvest, baptizing twenty-one precious souls! The wife was a sister of the college president who opposed public evangelism.

One couple had come every night. She had grown up a church member but had left the church more than forty years before. Her husband had never been a member. During the final call on the last night of the meetings, I removed my lapel microphone, and while Camille continued to play the organ softly, I walked down the aisle to the back row, where they were sitting. I leaned over the woman's shoulder and said, "I've been praying that you would make your decision tonight." She shook her head emphatically and said No.

I started to return to the front, but halfway there the Holy Spirit spoke to me through a strong impression: "You didn't ask the man." Feeling very foolish, I turned around, went back to the husband, and said, "I've been praying for you also. Wouldn't you like to give your heart to Jesus and become a part of His church?"

"Yes, I would," he said.

"You would?" his wife exclaimed.

"Yes," he replied. "I've been waiting for you."

She responded, "And I've been waiting for you."

They stood and embraced each other in a beautiful hug. Then, hand-in-hand, they walked down the aisle.

The next week the college president who'd said evangelism was dead had the great privilege of baptizing his sister and his favorite brother-in-law. Evangelism was alive and well in New England!

Bud Roberts, pastor in Taunton, Massachusetts, requested that we hold a series in his church, one of the large churches in the conference. Support for our ministry was beginning to grow. The next few years were filled with challenges, but it was a glorious time of soul winning.

The college president never apologized to me, nor did he have to. He often shook my hand, looked into my eyes, and told me how thrilled he was that his sister and brother-in-law were now active in the church. That was better than an apology. I knew he was now supporting public evangelism.

He was also a member of the conference committee. Whenever I would make a budget request, someone would usually try to cut it. Then the college president would make a strong speech of support, saying, "Give the man what he needs to do his work," and the request would almost always pass. Some of the ministers on the committee told me later, "You have a real friend on the committee." I knew who they were talking about. In time, even the conference treasurer became a firm supporter, and in retirement, he has become very active in public evangelism himself!

When we're attacked, we're usually inclined to defend ourselves. We should instead turn the matter over to the Lord, praying for our enemies as Jesus instructed us. He has ways of winning the battle that we've never imagined.

So, when you are attacked, "cover up" and wait on the Lord. He will come through for you. And keep on keeping on!

CHAPTER EIGHT

WHEN YOU ARE EMBARRASSED

My fiftieth birthday was a time of reflection. Camille asked if I wanted a party, and I replied that I would prefer spending an afternoon with her at the Texas state fair. We had a great time looking at the exhibits, eating corn on the cob, and doing all the things that adults enjoy at a fair, far from the midway and the rides.

As I contemplated the previous fifty years, numerous memories arose. Some of them concerned things that had happened right there on those fairgrounds. I remembered all the times we'd been there with our children and how much they had enjoyed themselves. I also remembered the times my parents had taken my brother Paul and me to this fair when we were young, making the hundred-mile trip from Tyler on a two-lane road. We'd leave early in the morning and finally pull back in our driveway late at night.

Later, when we moved to Dallas and I was attending Dallas Junior Academy, we lived close enough to make several trips to the fair during the three weeks it was held each year. I especially enjoyed the Joey Chitwood Daredevil show, with its star driver, Dapper Dan Fleanor. What a thrill for all the students at our school when Dapper Dan showed up in one of the show's painted cars to visit his parents. In their retirement years, Mr. and Mrs. Fleanor were serving as the custodians of the school and church. After Dapper Dan's visit, we treated the Fleanors, who were wonderful people, with a whole lot more respect!

In those days, I never had very much money, so a trip to the fair meant doing mostly the free stuff. I didn't spend much time on the midway where the rides were located, though sometimes I stayed to watch others ride, which was very entertaining in itself!

The year I was in the tenth grade was an exception to that. Dan Buckingham, my old friend from Tyler, had come to Dallas to attend DJA and was living with the Marvin and Minnie Stark family, whose house was close to the fairgrounds. Dan and I rode the city bus to the stop a block or so from the entrance. As we got off the bus, we saw a great opportunity. A nearby business was closing for the day, and its employees were driving out of the parking lot.

The official parking lots for the fair were on the far side of the fairgrounds. People who had businesses or homes within five or six blocks of the fair's entrance would rent parking spaces in their parking lots or their yards. When the fair closed for the day, it was much easier to exit from these smaller lots than from the big official lot.

Dan and I seized the opportunity and began waving people into the parking lot of the business. We charged $1 per car—a good price for such a convenient location. In just a few minutes, the lot was filled. We split the twenty-five dollars and headed to the midway feeling rich! The questionable ethics of what we'd done didn't dawn on us at the time.

On the way home from my birthday visit to the fair, I made a decision. I would step down as pastor of the Arlington Church and move on to another chapter of my life. The Lord had blessed my ministry in Arlington, and I was ready to make a move. So, in October, I told the board I would step down on January 1, giving them several months to form a search committee and work with the conference to find a replacement.

However, the Lord wasn't ready for me to make that move just yet. The search committee looked at many possibilities, but it couldn't reach a decision. I kept telling them my decision was final and that I would stick by the date. On the Sabbath before the January 1 deadline, the chair of the search committee, Dr. Bill Perryman, our head elder and a giant of a man in my eyes, told me he wanted to give a report of the search committee to the church at the close of my sermon that day.

Dr. Perryman went to the podium and read a carefully worded statement that in essence said the search committee had discussed names from all over the nation. They felt there was only one candidate who fit their needs at this time, and this was their current pastor, Jim Gilley.

The congregation broke into applause, which became a standing ovation that went on and on and on for what felt like an eternity. I strongly suspect that Bill and a few others had orchestrated the standing ovation, because it didn't stop until I said I would stay as pastor. I did stay for another three plus years. Those last three years were very rewarding. In addition to the continued growth of that church—the membership of which grew from about three hundred when I became their pastor to one thousand after seven years of ministry—we began an outreach to the Soviet Union. Our church members were very much a part of that outreach, both financially and through their participation. Eventually, we saw more than ten thousand baptisms in Ukraine and more than twenty churches organized in eight citywide efforts in the cities of Kiev, Odessa, Kharkiv, and Dnipropetrovs'k. So, the Lord's timing was best—as it always is!

By the end of those three years, however, I knew I should move on. This time I chaired the committee that searched for my replacement. We soon concluded that Pastor Mike Tucker was our man.

Pastor Tucker had been the pastor of the Burleson church only a few miles from Arlington. He was taking a leave of absence, and we had a hard time coaxing him back into pastoral ministry. We started by getting him to join me as a copastor. A year later, on my last Sabbath as pastor, the church voted Mike and Gayle Tucker into membership. That vote brought our membership to exactly one thousand.

What a ministry Mike and Gayle have had there! For nearly twelve years, they've served that congregation. It has continued to grow and flourish and now has about sixteen hundred members. In addition, the North American Division has asked Mike to add to his pastoral ministry the role of speaker-director of the *Faith for Today* telecast. The Lord has led!

After I resigned from Arlington, the Southwestern Union Conference asked me to become the evangelist, church-growth director, and evangelism coordinator of the union. For the previous twenty-five years, I had worked for the church on a one-dollar-a-year basis. I had my own business, which paid my salary. The employees of the business would be the first to tell you that my church work occupied the great majority of my time and that even the phone calls I handled during the day weighed heavily on the church side. However, the union committee—at the insistence especially of the president of the Arkansas-Louisiana Conference, Pastor Bill Woodruff—said they wanted me to be a regular full-time employee. They'd pay me the standard salary, but they didn't want me to continue working elsewhere. This is as it should be with a full-time employee.

Of course, taking this position under these conditions meant taking a very big cut in salary. I always told everyone that working for the church without pay was not as big a sacrifice as working for the church with pay! The full-time employees were the ones making the big sacrifice. And, with the exception of the health and retirement benefits, this is true. However, as one gets closer to retirement, these benefits become very important!

One of the first assignments I had was to hold a series of evangelistic meetings in one of the churches in the union. However, just before I was to go there, the pastor of that church took a position elsewhere. There had been some strain with the conference leadership. The president had now retired, and even though the pastor had left, the church had suffered some wounds that still hadn't healed. So, the new conference president called and told me he thought it best to cancel the series.

The cancellation of a series puts a big hole in the evangelist's schedule. I was anxious to conduct the series, so I proposed that I become pastor of the church for three months. I would take a month to prepare the church for the series, a month to hold the evangelistic meetings, and a month to do "follow-up." Perhaps by that time, the church would have a new pastor. He could join me for the last few weeks, and we would make a smooth transition. It was a brilliant plan, or so I thought! The conference president went along with the plan with some reservation, and I was off to the church.

I arrived in town on Friday afternoon and checked in to a modest local motel with my wife, Camille. She stayed in the motel with her book bag full of reading material, which is her companion for those hours she often waits for me while I'm in meetings. I hurried over to the church for a meeting with the elders and members of the church board, where we would talk about the plans for the next few months.

I believed this small church, which was clearly visible from the freeway, had great promise. So, I was really excited and started the meeting with the expectation of being warmly welcomed, of making some new friends and renewing an old friendship of a fellow who had roomed with a friend of mine in academy. I felt they certainly would have heard of the success that I had been a part of in the Arlington church and would be happy I was there.

Please understand, I give the Lord all the credit for the success I've been a part of. However, a woman prominent in church affairs in the Texas Conference once said to me, "I hope you don't think you are the reason that the Arlington church has grown." I answered, "Of course not, but I could have run them off!" Sometimes the most important thing a pastor can do is to avoid being so obnoxious that he runs everyone off—a few maybe, but not everyone!

Anyway, I was excited about the potential of this church and feeling very good about being there. I was letting all of this show and not holding anything back, which C. C. Blackburn had told me I should do. Blackburn, my old friend whom we all called Captain, was a former teacher, advisor, and mentor. He had told me that when I'm happy and relaxed, I come off as cocky. He said I'm the only person he knows who is most appealing, personality-wise, when I'm down, sad, hurt, or depressed.

To my shock, the elders of the church told me most emphatically that they did not want my services. They said I was too old (fifty-three!) to appeal to their church. They didn't want me to conduct an evangelistic series. They didn't want me to be their interim pastor. They wanted me to pack up and go home! I must have been very appealing as I left, because I was very discouraged!

I went to the motel and told Camille, "Let's put our stuff in the car and go home right now."

"Well," she reasoned with me, "we should spend the night, since we've already paid for the motel. And you really should go ahead and preach at the church tomorrow since your name is in the bulletin."

When You Are Embarrassed

"No way!" I protested. "You don't know how they talked to me. They don't want me! They were certainly very clear on that subject. They can do the service themselves!"

"Why don't you be bigger than that," she appealed. "Why don't you go over there tomorrow morning, and preach your heart out. Then we'll get in the car, shake the dust from our feet as the Bible says, and go home."

I knew from the meeting I had just attended that staying was a waste of time, but I told her I'd think about it.

All night I tossed and turned. The next morning we packed the car, checked out of the motel, and went to the church. I intentionally went late, but still got there too early. Within a few minutes of arriving, I felt I'd done the wrong thing by coming. The reception was cold. The looks I received clearly said, "What are you doing here? Didn't you get the message last night?"

The stress gave me a case of diarrhea. I ran to the bathroom. While I sat there, I prayed, "Lord, help me overcome these feelings of rejection." The prayer time renewed my spirit, and I was ready to pour myself into preaching the sermon. I was going to do everything I could to make a good impression and to make the church members wish they'd wanted me to hold the evangelistic series. However, I thought to myself, *I'm going straight back home for good after the benediction!*

The elders and I marched onto the platform to begin the service. When the time for the invocation came, I stepped up to the pulpit without hesitation, leaned heavily forward, and began: "Dear heavenly Father—" The pulpit was adjustable, and evidently, the pin that supported the top wasn't placed properly. So when I leaned on the pulpit, the top collapsed. The resulting bang, amplified by my microphone, sounded like a shotgun blast. Everyone in the church jumped—especially me! I thought someone had started shooting at me. I knew they didn't want me, but I hadn't thought they'd go that far!

I'm sure I paused for only a second or so, but it seemed an eternity before I could regain my composure and continue with the prayer. So much for the good impression. I felt like a complete fool!

The service continued normally until we came to the morning prayer. I was wearing my very best, new, black suit, which was a little too tight for me. As we knelt, I had a decision to make. Should I unbutton the coat as I was kneeling for prayer, or should I leave it buttoned like the other, thin guys on the platform were doing? Trying, again, to make a good impression, I made the wrong choice. I left my suit coat buttoned. Just as my knee touched the carpet, the button popped off, flying several feet to my right. I was sure a number of people in the congregation saw what had happened, because I heard a few snickers.

When it was time for me to preach the sermon, I arose and began. Toward the end of my sermon, as I was preaching my heart out, I felt something beneath my feet. When I had gone into the restroom before the service, I had covered the toilet seat with toilet paper. Apparently, a piece had stuck to my leg. It had worked loose, fallen down my pant leg, and now was stuck on my shoe. I was dragging it around in plain sight of everyone in the church! What little dignity I had left was gone for sure.

That's it! I thought. *What a way to go. Total self-destruction.*

Which it was! But the Lord works in mysterious ways, His wonders to perform. He can use us best when self has been destroyed. As I went to the door, the people were so warm—so totally different than they had been before the service. The elders waited around until everyone left and then asked if they could talk to me. I was hoping it was not about the toilet paper! They said they had reconsidered, and I could hold the meeting in their church.

Camille and I stayed, and the next three months were a great time with a great bunch of people, many of whom became our friends. The harvest was not large numerically, but the wife of one of the young adults in the church became a member, and she alone would have been worth the three months of ministry. When our time was up, the elders asked if I would consider staying to be their pastor. What a change!

The Lord specializes in turnarounds in marriages, churches, families, businesses, and ministries! He knows how to make success out of failure, life out of death, warmth from cold, and to take a very embarrassing situation and turn it to His glory. What a God! What a Lord! What a Savior! He, and He alone, is worthy of our praise.

Keep on keeping on with Jesus—even when you are so embarrassed that you can't face anyone else!

CHAPTER NINE

WHEN YOU ARE FIRED

It was a beautiful fall Sunday in Amarillo, Texas, where I was holding evangelistic meetings. The temperature was nearly perfect, and most people couldn't resist getting out of their houses—which made my job of visitation more difficult. I had set a goal of visiting at least twelve families before meeting time that evening.

The first go-around, only four were at home. I kept cruising by the other homes, seeing if perchance a car was in the driveway or if there was any indication they had returned. Each time I made the circuit, I picked up another visit or two. By the time I needed to go to the church to make my final preparations for the meeting, I had seen nearly all of those who were on my list.

I was finishing running through the slides for the night's program when one of the church members told me I had a telephone call. My friend, Max Trevino, who at the time was the treasurer of the Southwestern Union Conference, was calling. He was more businesslike than usual, which told me that this was an official phone call. But I couldn't determine the nature of the call.

"Hold a minute, Jim," Max said. "Cyril wants to talk to you."

He was referring to Cyril Miller, the Southwestern Union Conference president and my immediate boss.

"What does he want to talk to me about?" I quizzed.

"I'll let him tell you," Max said.

I couldn't read his tone. I could hear the buzz of people talking in the background, as if a group were talking after a meeting was over. I could also hear Max calling for Cyril. Max still had his cell phone to his ear, so I took one more try at finding out what this was about.

"Max," I said, "what's going on? Am I in some kind of trouble?"

"You might say that," he said, with one of his patented laughs, which sounds a little like a goose's squawk. "It's Cyril's place to tell you. I'm trying to get him to the phone now."

I was even more confused than before. I imagined them to be in the lobby of the union office, and I kept racking my brain. *What are they doing there on Sunday?* I thought.

When Cyril finally got to the phone, he greeted me warmly and asked if I were sitting down. When I told him No, he suggested that I do just that. "Jim," he said, "you have just been elected president of the Arkansas-Louisiana Conference."

I had been so focused on the evangelistic series I was conducting that I had completely forgotten that the Arkansas-Louisiana Conference triennial session was meeting that day in Shreveport, Louisiana.

A few weeks before, I had pulled a trick on my friend, Denton James, who was the publishing director for the union. Cyril had played along with me, and now the thought came to me that Denton was getting me back and had solicited Cyril's help.

"This is a joke, isn't it Cyril? Denton's put you up to this."

"It's no joke," Cyril answered seriously. "Furthermore, I need your answer right now. These people need to drive home knowing they have a president."

I offered up a quick prayer: *Lord, do You want me to do this?*

Quite honestly, evangelism has always been my first love. It's the most difficult work I've ever done, but it's also the most rewarding. The meeting I was conducting was going reasonably well; if it had been going phenomenally well, I would have said No without hesitation. But lately, I had been doing some serious thinking. I had begun to wonder whether evangelism was "a young man's game," as an old preacher had told me once. I had also looked at my picture on the handbill and asked myself, "Would I get into my car and drive across town to a strange church to listen to that old guy?" I didn't like the answer I got. Perhaps it was time for me to move off the playing field and into a coach's position—supporting and training younger ministers in the grueling work of soul winning. I knew there was no position where you could affect the ministries of young pastors more effectively than as a conference president.

I hadn't campaigned for the position of president, and no one had campaigned for it on my behalf. I hadn't even remembered there was an election that day. So I concluded that this call was truly the Lord's will. I also knew that if within a few days I felt that the Lord didn't want me to take the position, it would certainly be acceptable for me to change my mind. So I told Cyril, "Yes. I'll do my best to do a good job."

Cyril thanked me and then gave the phone back to Max. Evidently Cyril then made his way back to the podium to tell the delegates that the president they had elected had accepted. The great majority, more than the 66.67 percent required by the constitution, were happy. Some were very unhappy. Many of those who were unhappy had opposed the prior president and had helped bring about his loss of the nomination and thus his decision to resign and retire. These members had someone else in mind. They hadn't wanted any of "Cyril's boys," as they referred to the three names Cyril had put into nomination.

I told Camille about the election, but neither of us had much time to consider it then because it was time to start the evangelistic meeting. I think I was talking about the state of the dead that night. I must have preached like a zombie because my mind was on the conversation I'd just had with Cyril.

To save money for the conference, we were staying in a cottage Dr. Harlan Wilson had maintained behind his house for his mother when she was alive. The Wilsons now used it for guests, and we were enjoying the quiet country location. However, that night it wasn't quiet. The phone nearly rang off of the hook with one call after another. Some calls were from friends who wanted to congratulate us. Others were from people we didn't know. They had been delegates to the meeting and were calling either to get acquainted or to get in an early request for something they wanted the conference to do under this new administration. Each would apologize for calling so late, but they would add they knew I was up because they had been trying for a long time and the line had been busy.

When the phone finally quit ringing, I sat for a long time in a recliner in the little cottage, thinking about what a day it had been. I thought about the thirty-four years Camille and I had been married. I thought about all the different phases of our lives—from teaching school in Montana, to college and seminary in Michigan, to evangelism in Massachusetts, the three M's. Then I thought back to my native Texas, and a combined life of business and ministry, being active in Adventist Laymen's Services and Industries (ASI), and then the decision to leave business behind and devote all our time to ministry. And now I was being asked to be the president of a conference—something I had thought would never happen. I felt sure I wouldn't forget a single minute of that day. I had no idea that within a few weeks I would wish that day had never come.

When I awoke the next morning, I realized it had not been a dream. I had been elected. I called the union president, and he counseled me to go to Shreveport the next day and meet with the conference staff. I bought tickets and made the trip. I had a list of things to talk over with the former president. The number one item on the list was a request that he stay with the conference on a stipend and remain as an advisor to me. This was number eight on his list. He agreed to stay and work in the trust department. Taking this position was his choice. He also agreed to keep all the conference office computers humming, a hobby of his that really helped the conference. Other presidents warned me it was not wise to keep a former president around, but that was one decision I never regretted.

When we wrapped up the evangelistic series in Amarillo, we prepared to go to Shreveport to assume our duties there. At that point, I still didn't feel like I was a conference president. Then I received a call from one of the pastors. He asked for permission to miss the combined workers meeting and prayer conference that was scheduled to begin soon in the Gentry church. I listened to his reason, thought it unreasonable, and kindly denied his request. I told him I looked forward to seeing him at the meeting. I remember thinking, *That's my first decision as a conference president. I'm starting to feel more presidential.*

Then the phone rang again. It was Cyril Miller. He said he had just received an unsigned letter that was being circulated in the Arkansas-Louisiana Conference. It contained many serious charges against me. Suddenly, I was sick to my stomach and feeling very unpresidential! I'd not asked for the job, but I certainly didn't want to lose it before I could even get started just because of an anonymous letter. I told Cyril that I didn't think anyone took unsigned letters seriously. He said he thought I should look at this one and asked me to come to the union office so he could give me a copy.

I went, and when I read the letter, I could see why he was taking it seriously. The letter contained just enough fact, just enough truth—though ingeniously twisted—to make it believable. For instance, I had been in business in the area for twenty-five years. During that time, I'd had to fire some people. One had stolen over $200,000 worth of inventory from my company, and he had sold this stolen merchandise to our customers. Other people had encouraged me to turn the matter over to the police, but I chose not to. This man did his best to poison the community toward me. He told them how I had fired him with "no heart" just before Christmas. His grown children hated me until years later when they finally learned the truth. The letter contained this man's stories and the tales of others, who, for one reason or another, we had to let go. They were now getting even.

There were other charges that were difficult to answer. I drove a Mercedes-Benz, which apparently made people wonder about my financial priorities. Of course, the letter's author didn't tell the whole story. I had bought the car in Europe when the dollar was strong and had driven it for thirteen years and put more than three hundred thousand miles on it, all the while getting great mileage from its diesel engine. Later, when I sold that car and bought a Toyota that actually cost me more money, people thought I was being prudent. Try to figure that one out!

The letter made a big deal about my having a gold Rolex watch. A friend had gotten it for me wholesale some twenty-five years before, when gold was artificially held at thirty-five dollars per ounce. Now it was worth about ten times that much, which greatly increased the value of the watch. It appeared to be extravagant, but it wasn't. Still the watch had to go. So goodbye Rolex, hello again Timex. One "-ex" or the other really doesn't make any difference does it? They both tell what time it is.

The letter also named other people whom I had supposedly hurt.

When I read the letter, I asked myself whether I would believe it if it were written about someone else. I had to say, yes, without answers, I would.

Cyril showed me the letter on Wednesday, and the conference committee wanted to meet with me the next Monday evening to discuss the matter. That meant I had to get answers right away. I had no idea how to handle this, but Vern Carner called me with advice. At the time, he was the assistant to Steve Gifford, president of the Texas Conference.

Vern said I should simply contact each person mentioned in the letter and ask them to respond with the truth. I did, and I was amazed at how quickly they faxed or brought me written letters, setting the record straight. Many of them were very upset that they had been misquoted or the circumstances of the situation mentioned had been greatly exaggerated or totally distorted. Their letters gave me new confidence.

By Friday afternoon, everyone had answered, and the letters were printed and collated. Then began a very difficult Sabbath. A very disturbing dream awakened me early that morning. I dreamed I was in a battle. It seemed to be a spiritual battle, but it was being fought on a real battlefield. Was it the great controversy?

Satan was the enemy, and I longed to fight him. However, when I went to the battlefield, I was turned back because I had been wounded long ago. I had kept the scars hidden under my shirt, but well-meaning people on the side of good wouldn't let me fight because of those old wounds. They turned me back from the front lines. They were harsh and mean, and they would have done me harm if I had tried to continue to battle. These people tore away my clothing and revealed the scars. The enemy seemed to be using them to keep me from reaching the Great Commander.

I woke up with hot tears rolling down my cheeks. I felt as discouraged as I've ever been in my entire life. I had planned to go to church that day—to keep a stiff upper lip, to show a strong exterior, to walk tall, with head lifted high, but I couldn't. I felt totally defeated. Camille and I almost never miss church, but we spent that Sabbath in prayer, Bible study, and heart searching. Should we continue or simply throw in the towel?

It's not worth it. Let them have their way. Life is too short. All these thoughts kept coming to mind. Camille, supportive as always, told me that she was with me no matter what decision I made.

Friends called and encouraged us. Then, late in the afternoon, the doorbell rang. Walter and Jackie Wright had come to lend their support. The Lord had sent them at just the right time. Walter encouraged me not to give up. He said, "They are counting on you to quit. Don't do it. Fool them. Hang in there."

Cyril Miller and Max Trevino were in Washington, D.C., attending Annual Council at the General Conference headquarters. On Monday, I received word that Cyril couldn't return from the Annual Council because of a very important item that was to come before the committee that day. He was calling to ask that I postpone the meeting with the conference committee. I made a very unwise decision. I decided that we should go ahead with the meeting without him. A friend who was advising me had convinced me I had to stand on my own without the union president's help; that he was as much a target of my enemies as I was. So, I insisted that the meeting go ahead as scheduled.

Camille and I drove to Shreveport and met the committee for the first time. I was very impressed with the caliber of people who were on the committee. I immediately liked every one of them. I knew that if I had the chance to work with them, we would get along together famously and could advance the Lord's work together. I could feel it deep in my soul. But for the first time, I began to fear that I would never have the opportunity to work with them.

I went through the letter with the committee. I gave them the documents that refuted the untruths, and I straightened out, as best I could, the half-truths. I also told them things about me that the letter hadn't mentioned but that I felt they had the right to know, especially in light of the controversy. The principal item had taken place nearly thirty years before, and I had, as nearly as possible, made it right. Then I entertained questions and answered each question honestly and forthrightly.

The anonymous letter had not mentioned the more than ten years I had served the Texas Conference as evangelist without pay while running a Christian business. It didn't state that I had served as vice president of the Southwestern Union chapter of ASI, had been on the conference, union, division, and General Conference committees as well as on the board of the Review and Herald Publishing Association.

The letter didn't tell of the seven years I pastored the Arlington church, again without pay. It didn't say that during that time the church had grown from three hundred members to a thousand members. It didn't indicate that, as the senior pastor, I had spent thousands of hours visiting in hospitals and homes and countless hours in board and committee meetings. Nor did it mention the work I had done in Ukraine, which, combined with the efforts of others, resulted in more than ten thousand baptisms—again, while I was not on the payroll. The committee members asked about these things, and I answered, giving the Lord all the glory. I could tell from the faces of the committee members that the great majority of them were with me.

I assured the committee members that I wanted to be their president only if they had confidence in me and that I would abide by their decision. In doing so, I made another mistake. The constitution required a 66.6 percent vote for a president to be removed from office. However, when I had said I would abide by the committee's decision, I had taken that provision away and had made the matter subject to a simple majority vote.

I was ready to call for the vote, but one member of the opposition said he wanted me to leave the room so the committee could discuss the matter freely. At this point the union president's presence would have been critical. This is when my decision to go ahead without him hurt me. No one was left in the room to protect me in any way; I had no one "covering my back."

So, Camille and I waited quietly in the president's office while those who were determined that I be removed began their presentations. At first I was optimistic, but as the time lengthened, I was sure what the answer would be.

Finally, the secretary of the conference and the treasurer came to talk to us. Both of these men felt that the unrest in the conference over this issue would be impossible to overcome, and they honestly let me know they had joined with those who voted against my continuing. The vote was nine to seven against my remaining as president. Even if I had been allowed to vote, which the constitution would have permitted, the tally would have been nine to eight. Of course, if the two officers had voted with me, the vote would have been ten to seven in my favor. But, as the old east Texas saying goes, "If 'ifs' and 'buts' were candy and nuts, we'd all have a merry Christmas." So, I was out.

We returned to the committee room, and I told the committee members that I knew this had been a difficult decision and that even though I didn't fully agree with it, I certainly understood it. I told them I wished I had been fortunate enough to have worked with them. I suggested that we have a circle of prayer. We joined arms and I prayed for them, after which I went around the circle and either shook hands with or hugged every member. Then Camille and I walked out of that beautiful colonial conference office.

A bright October moon floated overhead. Its light shone through pine trees whose branches were being stirred by a gentle breeze. It was a beautiful night, but we felt so alone, disappointed, and rejected. I'm not one who cries easily even when I need to and should, such as at funerals of loved ones. My brother Paul used to tell me I would never be a great preacher because I couldn't cry like _ _ _ _ _ _, and he would name some famous preachers who could cry at the drop of a hat. But as we drove away that night, a few tears found their way down my cheeks. Our drive back to Arlington was long and lonely.

The next two months were awful. The conference committee had appointed themselves as a search committee and announced a new constituency meeting to be held in sixty days, the minimum time required for notification of a constituency meeting. Meanwhile, I began to try to put my life back together as the union evangelist and church-growth specialist. I tried to rebuild my evangelistic schedule, having cancelled the meetings that had been planned when I had been elected president.

Email and Web sites had just become very popular within the church. There was one—now defunct—Web site named Adventist Forum CompuServe, where all the gossip of the church was displayed by anyone who wanted to post it. My reputation was completely demolished on these sites—what was left of it, that is! So, Camille and I suffered through two months of misery, unspeakable and indescribable.

One morning, Carl Phipps and Michael Cuilla, two friends who helped me in evangelism as volunteers, brought me a plaque. That plaque still hangs in my office today as a symbol of friendship. Carl and Michael had placed Psalm 109 on the plaque. They said, "We're praying Psalm 109 down on your enemies."

When I read that psalm, I said, "Don't do that! No one deserves that."

Read that psalm! David must have been having more than simply a "bad day." When God said, "David is a man after My own heart," I believe He was speaking of David's tendency to forgive even his enemies. But Psalm 109 communicates anything but a forgiving spirit. It shows that the Lord can forgive us even for the times we've been unwilling to forgive, if we confess this sin.

In the days before the special constituency meeting, Cyril Miller was traveling. Sometime earlier, his beloved wife Marian had lost a long and painful bout with cancer. Cyril and a college sweetheart, Joyce, had become reacquainted and had married. They went on their honeymoon just before the constituency meeting, so I hadn't been able to visit with Cyril until the night before that meeting.

At a reception for the newlyweds at the library at Southwestern, we talked for a few minutes. Someone at the reception had told me he thought I might be re-elected as president the next day. I was just as sure it wouldn't happen, but I told Cyril what this person had said. Cyril told me there wasn't a chance in the world that would happen. He couldn't think of any president in North America who had ever been voted out and then returned to office.

All union departmental directors, of which I was one, were expected to attend constituency meetings. We were to hand out, collect, and count ballots and be available for any other duties that might be needed. I asked Cyril if I might be excused from attending the meeting; I told him I didn't feel it was appropriate that I be there. He told me that I was not excused. I had to be able to serve in all parts of the union if I was to work on the union staff. I knew he was right. I had been excused while I was holding that crusade in Amarillo, but I had no excuse this time. I knew I had to go and face the music.

The next morning I left for Shreveport. A lot of other people were driving the same route, but even though I hinted to some, no one invited me to ride with them. One even flat turned me down. I felt like a leper. Then Vern Carner called and asked if he could ride with me. I was glad for the company.

As we neared Shreveport, I came under the conviction that it was not proper for me to attend the meeting. As we entered the city, I stopped at a Red Roof Inn (because that was the cheapest motel!) and checked in. I told Vern to take the car and to tell Max Trevino, the union treasurer, where I was. I told him that if he believed I should be there, he should call me and I would come. Then I stretched out on the bed and fell fast asleep. I hadn't been able to sleep much the night before, and now I was exhausted. I was sure it was over for me.

In the meantime, things were happening at the session. Pastor Don Fortner gave the devotional, choosing as his subject King David. He said that God chose David even though God knew in advance that David would make many mistakes. He noted that later, God said of David that he had done only that which was right in His sight.

I don't know everything that happened at the session, and I'm sure many people came to my defense and should be mentioned. But

I am going to mention only three: pastors Rudy Hein and Mike Tomblinson, and Mike's wife, Rhonda. After the delegates made their speeches, Rhonda moved that they rescind the conference committee's decision to remove me from the presidency. Someone seconded the motion, and the vote carried by a wide margin. With that one vote, the impossible had happened. I was returned to office.

Max called the motel, told me that I had been reinstated, and asked if I would serve. I said, "Max, I'll have to think about it."

He replied, "Don't give me that nonsense. A lot of your friends really put themselves on the line for you today."

I really didn't have a choice. Even though I no longer wanted to be president, I knew I had to if I was ever to redeem my reputation. So I accepted.

However, the battle wasn't over yet. The opposition made one more appeal for my resignation, at the first conference committee I chaired. The constituency delegates had instructed them not to vote me out again. They said that if the committee did, they would vote out the entire committee. But this did not keep the opposition from doing everything they could to get me to quit. Don Jacobsen, the assistant to Al McClure, the president of the North American Division, spoke to the committee in support of my remaining. Cyril's and Max's strong support reassured me as well.

So I went to work. Camille and I got into the car and made a whirlwind tour around the conference, putting over eight thousand miles on our car in less than six weeks. We went to every district and visited with each pastor. We saw nearly every church and church school so that when situations came up and a property was discussed, I could talk about the building or piece of land from personal experience.

There was some strain between the three conference officers—the events of the past two months had taken their toll. However, within a few months we were a team, pulling hard together for common goals. We determined to eliminate the conference debt, increase the tithe, increase the baptisms, build a new boys' dormitory at the academy, and accomplish other worthwhile endeavors. I loved working with those two men, and I loved working with the conference committee, and the Lord blessed. In addition, the members of the conference and their pastors could not have been more supportive. Today, they are some of the best friends we have.

About six weeks after I was reinstated, I attended the conference presidents' retreat at Pine Springs Ranch in southeastern California. Every president there knew what I had been through. One even came to me and said, "I can't believe you accepted that position again. You have so much going against you. There's no way you can pull out of it."

At our first meeting during the retreat, we went around the circle, each president giving his name and then telling how long he had served and whether he was in his first, second, or third term or more. When it was my turn, the room became very quiet, and every eye looked my way. I said, "I'm Jim Gilley. I've been a president for six weeks, and I'm in my second term." The place erupted in laughter. Sometimes, the best way to handle a difficult situation is head on and with a little humor. After that, the group made me feel at home. During the seven years that I attended those retreats, people would often tease me with the question, "How many terms have you served?"

Three years after I was elected conference president, it was time for another constituency meeting and the re-election of officers. I was apprehensive, of course. But at that meeting, on April 27, 1997, I was re-elected by secret ballot with 96.55 percent of the vote. The entire group broke into a spontaneous standing ovation. Again in 2000, I was re-elected by more than 96 percent of the delegates.

In 2001, Camille and I were attending a meeting of the pastors and conference and union staff of the Southwestern Union Conference. I always took those from our conference out to eat at least once during a meeting like that. The meal was to be mostly a time of fellowship, but I had planned a short program: a few introductions and some remarks. We had invited the union president, Max Trevino, formerly the union treasurer, and his wife, Betty, and our division president, Don Schneider, and his wife, Marti.

Much to my surprise, when I was about to begin my short program, they had me sit down. Our conference pastors had planned a program of their own, honoring Camille and me. Don Schneider told me later that he had never seen a sitting president honored by his workers like that. He said, "They usually reserve something like that for a farewell!" He told us this the next morning, when he asked us if we would join him at the division as a general vice president for media, ministerial, stewardship, and evangelism, subject to the North American Division's Committee's vote. We told him we loved it where we were, but that without a house (it had burned a couple of months before), this might be an opportune time for a move, if that's what the Lord wanted.

A few weeks later, Don called and issued the official call. The committee had just voted for me to join his team. What a privilege it has been to work with such a caring and capable person! I felt totally inadequate to fill the shoes of the retiring vice president, who had held the position for the past six years—I was to try to take the place of Cyril Miller, one of the most intelligent and creative individuals I have ever known. Honestly, I've never felt equal to the task!

Romans 8:28 says "all things work together for good" (KJV). I don't think this means that we will always be happy with the process or even the results. But I believe with all my heart that this verse means that if we trust our Lord and ask Him to take each experience we face in life—good, bad, or just plain horrible—and work it to His glory and our growth and good, He will do just that.

Don't miss the blessing that is in every challenge that comes your way. Don't let any defeat put you down for the count. Hold on to Jesus Christ. Don't just touch the hem of His garment, grab on to it and hold on for dear life, and He will bring you through.

Keep on keeping on even when they tell you, "You're fired"!

CHAPTER TEN

WHEN YOUR CHURCH
LETS YOU DOWN

Not long ago, Jerry Lutz, pastor of the Spencerville, Maryland, church where I'm a member, had an unfortunate fall on the ice, breaking four of his facial bones. This was a very debilitating injury for a preacher—he couldn't talk! Rob Vandeman, a former pastor of Spencerville and currently executive secretary of the Chesapeake Conference, filled in for Jerry one week. His subject was "Dinner at the Homesick Café."

Pastor Vandeman told about an eating establishment in Carolina that was located near a military base. The proprietors decided that they would serve favorite dishes from around the country: enchiladas and tacos from the Southwest; three-alarm chili from Texas; grits and gravy from the deep South; Boston baked beans, tortellini, and spaghetti from the Northeast; and other favorites from various regions of the United States. The idea was that the young men and women stationed on the base could come in and order the kind of food that would remind them of home. The café was very successful!

I guess we all think of the favorite meals we had at home. The home in which I grew up wasn't vegetarian. In fact, I'm not sure I ever met a vegetarian until I was a teenager. My mother, younger brother Paul, and I were the only Adventists in our family, and we usually had a very simple meal after church on Sabbath. Our main meal was Sunday dinner. Mom really put on a feed! She prepared several chickens, which in my early years, we raised ourselves. Fried

chicken along with fresh homemade rolls, mounds of mashed pota-
toes and gravy, green beans and other vegetables, along with Mom's
limp salad, and topped off with her special pies—either lemon, choco-
late, or coconut meringue—made up our special meal. We loved those
Sunday dinners.

It wasn't until I married that I found out what a great blessing a
Sabbath meal can be. Camille took after her mom; she can put a vegetarian meal on the table that is delicious, nourishing, and healthy.
Camille and I are fortunate to have four of the greatest kids that any
parents could ever have. When our children were growing up, we
had some great family food traditions. On Friday nights, haystacks
were a regular. For Sabbath lunch, lasagna was the favorite. If Camille
prepared anything else, the kids would ask, "Where's the lasagna?" I
ran into one of our son John's friends, Jason Kindopp, not long ago.
He said, "I can still remember Sabbath dinner at the Gilleys' place,"
and he rattled off the menu, starting with the lasagna.

Another favorite was chili soup—sort of a vegetarian chili with
macaroni in it that is truly a soup, not a chili mac. And for breakfast,
Camille often made egg a la goldenrod. It still is a favorite, especially
with Jim Jr. He told Orville Iversen about it, and when Orville visited our home, he insisted that Camille fix that dish. I learned later
that his wife, Mary, had often made it for him, and it brought back
great memories of her.

The spiritual food of the home is even more important than the
physical food. Lifting Christ without being preachy. Having prayer
with each child each night, which we often found to be even more
effective than a collective family worship. (With all the comedians
we had in our home, our collective worships often degenerated into
gabfests!) We also, as a family, worked at sharing Jesus with people—
in our case, each child was a very important part of the evangelistic
team and had a specific job to perform. During the meetings, Jim Jr.
would run the computer; Maryann, the sound system; John, the spotlight; and Amy would help with tape duplication.

The church itself is a family, or at least it should be. As a pastor, I
have been in some very difficult homes with dysfunctional families.
Sometimes our churches are also dysfunctional. We should do our

very best to make them healthier. They will never be perfect, just as our homes aren't perfect. But we can make our churches safe places for those seeking spiritual growth.

Many of our churches have finally realized that "spiritual growth" is just that. We vary just as much as to where we are in the spiritual growth cycle as we do physically. Those churches that are jumping on people with faults and even sins soon find that they are emptying out! We all goof up. We should always be ready to extend a helping hand to others who are in spiritual need, because we never know when we'll need one extended to us! It has been my experience that those who are living lives of spiritual victory are tolerant of those with struggles; it's those who are covering secret sins who are hard on others who slip.

I know of a couple who were very hard on anyone with a problem. The husband was the head elder of a little church, and his wife was the treasurer. They were always ready to take problems to the church board and to place their fellow members under church censorship or to have them disfellowshiped. Those of us who have observed such things through the years weren't surprised when this couple's own problems burst into notice. The man had been having a longstanding affair with another church member, and his wife had embezzled thousands of dollars from the church through the many years that she had been treasurer. The little church closed due to the scandal.

Jesus said, " 'He who is without sin among you, let him throw a stone . . . first' " (John 8:7, NKJV). I believe that instead of casting stones, we should, like the Savior, seek to restore and save those who are lost.

When I was pastoring in Arlington, Texas, a woman came to me and said, "You don't preach on sin enough."

I'd heard that this woman had discouraged some of our young people by chiding them about their dress and other things, so I was ready to respond differently than she probably expected. "Oh," I said, "I'm not going to be preaching on sin. I think they have that one down pretty good. They're sinning more than they should. I want to talk to them about Jesus. He is the only way to life eternal."

A few weeks later, the woman said to me, "You need to preach about makeup."

I replied, "Not on your life—they're wearing too much already!"

I knew that this woman had cornered some of our young girls and gave them a speech that made them not want to return to church. She was running the young people off as fast as the Holy Spirit and I could draw them in. I knew I had to do something, so I said, "You know, our philosophy, as long as I am here, will be to let the Holy Spirit bring conviction on these things. I will preach Jesus and a strong relationship with Him, and in time, as they enter into a relationship with Him, there will be a change."

Then I added, "I really think you will feel a lot more at home at another church," and I named a church only a few miles away that she had often mentioned to me as a place where they "toe the line." I told her that I thought that church would work better for her.

She agreed with me and started going to the other church. We remained friendly, and when I would see her, she would tell me how happy she was. I would say, "That's great! Please tell the pastor hello for me." She was happy, and so were we!

Jesus, our Example, was easy on sinners. We see this in the lack of condemnation He showed toward the woman found committing adultery. We need to be hard on the Pharisees and legalists who accuse sinners. Usually, we do just the opposite. I don't mean that Jesus was easy on sin. No way! However, He knew sin was not just limited to the deeds of the flesh. He knew the sins that are most difficult to deal with are those of attitude, and that often, for that reason, we let those sins hamper the way we deal with people in need of spiritual help.

As a denomination, we must make our church homes warm, receptive, and nonjudgmental. In the mid 1990s, the North American Division sponsored a "Welcome Home" Sabbath. My childhood home church, in Tyler, Texas, where my oldest brother, Ed, is a member, invited me to preach the sermon that Sabbath. They also told me they planned to invite my brother John, who is a member of another denomination, to come and sing. He's a soloist in a three-hundred-member choir that sings to a fifteen-thousand-member congregation in a twenty-six-million-dollar worship center.

"You can ask him," I said, "but I doubt very seriously that he will come."

"Why?" Pastor Jim Ferguson asked.

I told him the following story. When John was about fourteen years old, he went to a theater to see a movie—*Old Yeller,* or some movie like that. The pastor saw John go into the theater, and the next day, between Sabbath School and the worship service, he cornered John outside the church near a water faucet where the few kids in the congregation went for a drink.

"John, did I see you go into a theater on the square yesterday?" the pastor asked.

"Yes, you did," John answered, truthfully.

I was standing by, listening intently to every word. *Boy, oh boy, John's in trouble. This is great!* I thought. To a little brother, six years younger, seeing an older sibling in an embarrassing situation was too good to be true!

"Do you promise me you will never go to a theater again?" the pastor asked.

"No, I couldn't make that promise," John answered. "I don't go very often, but I love dog and horse stories, and if they make a movie of *My Friend Flicka,* I'll probably go." John had loved the book *Black Beauty* and had also seen that movie, as there were no video rentals or TVs yet in our part of the world—in other words, no way that Adventists could see these kinds of things "legally" in those days.

The conversation over, the pastor went in to the church to conduct the worship service. After the closing prayer, he called the members into a special business session. He told them that he had witnessed John going into a movie theater the day before. He said he had visited with John, and John had not promised that he wouldn't go again. "So," he said, "I would like to entertain a motion that his membership be dropped."

Someone made the motion. It was seconded, and the entire church voted him out. This included my mother, who, for the unity of the church, voted—with tears running down her cheeks—with the other members. John got up and walked out of the church, vowing never to return. And young as I was, instead of being glad that my brother was in trouble, I realized that a terrible wrong had been committed.

Pastor Ferguson went to the church clerk's records and found in the minutes a description of the event. He told me it was surprisingly close to what I had described to him. He took the action to the church board. They decided, nearly fifty years after the event had taken place, to rescind the action. Pastor Ferguson wrote my brother John one of the most beautiful letters I have ever read. It not only told him the church board had rescinded the action, thereby restoring his membership if he so desired, but also asked for John's forgiveness. Not only the pastor but also every member of the church board had signed that letter.

That letter healed a great hurt; only eternity will tell all its consequences. That is the true spirit of "Home Coming." That is the true spirit of love that Christ would have us follow. "Turn the other cheek" means that we don't always have to be right and win every argument.

My friend and mentor Fordyce Detamore wrote a book called *Seeking His Lost Sheep*. In it he talks about all the thousands of people who have left the church because some member wronged them. He so wisely writes, "Don't try to defend the actions of a member of the church family, regardless of whether the wrong was real, imagined, or justified. Just simply say you are sorry. Apologize for the family. You are authorized as a church family member to do so."

Great memories. Great homes. That is what makes for great families. The same is true of our church families. I don't know whether it was the elder brother's attitude that drove the prodigal son from his home, but I suspect it may have contributed to his leaving. However, the elder brother didn't do anything to welcome the prodigal home, did he? If the elder brother had gotten his way, he would have driven the prodigal off again!

Don't let someone else's mistreatment of you drive you away from the church. Keep on keeping on with Jesus! And if you know someone who needs to come back, run like the father in Jesus' parable to welcome that person with not only open arms but also an open attitude of love.

CHAPTER ELEVEN

WHEN YOU HAVE A TRULY IMPOSSIBLE DREAM

When L. R. Conradi organized the first Seventh-day Adventist church in the United States among the Russian-Ukrainian immigrants of German descent, he noted the burden they felt for the country and the people they had left behind. Philip Reiswig, one of the members of that church, was old, he stuttered, and he had no money. But he wanted to return to his native land with the message of the three angels. So, in November 1883, as a self-supporting missionary with no help from his local church, the conference, or anyone else, he traveled back to the land he'd left. He faced great persecution from the authorities and the state church. However, in time, our church found its beginning in the land that was to become the Soviet Union.

The persecution from the state church largely subsided in 1917, when the Bolshevik revolution brought the Communists to power. For ten years or so, the church experienced phenomenal growth. Then the Communists began to apply restrictions. And when the war with Hitler ended, Joseph Stalin turned his attention to religion and declared war on all faiths—even the one that had been the state church. During the seventy-year reign of Communism, more than fifty million citizens of the Soviet Union were put to death, the majority of them during Stalin's rule.

By 1946, the Adventist Church in the Soviet Union was nearly extinct. The government had confiscated all church buildings. More than a hundred pastors had died in front of firing squads, and hundreds more were exiled to Siberia, never to be heard from again.

In Dnipropetrovs'k, a large manufacturing city on the Dnieper River in central Ukraine, an Adventist church that had once flourished had dwindled down to six faithful women members. The men had all been killed or exiled or had renounced their faith and embraced Communism.

These six women met in one another's homes each week. They varied the place of meeting carefully to avoid drawing the attention of their neighbors, who would most likely have reported them to receive a reward from the state. They had no Bibles, so they would recite texts from memory, pray, and whisper hymns softly, placing pillows in the windows to keep any sound from escaping the room where they worshiped. It was a very dark time for all believers, with no end in sight.

One Sabbath, one of the women, Daria Saveleuna Sologub, said she'd had a dream the night before. When she began to relate it, another woman, Daria Pavlovna, declared she'd had the very same dream. Daria Pavlovna picked up the narrative and finished relating the dream, and the two women confirmed that their dreams were identical.

The dreams carried a simple message. One day a man from America would preach in Dnipropetrovs'k. Thousands would attend the services, hundreds would be baptized, and the church in that city would again be strong. God would answer their prayers and reward their faithfulness.

You talk about an impossible dream! There was no way this could ever happen. In the first place, Christianity was illegal. And second, Dnipropetrovs'k was a "closed" city, a secret city. Many highly secret military products were manufactured there, including intercontinental ballistic missiles. Though the city had a population of about two million, it did not even appear on maps of the country. None of its citizens was allowed to have a telephone, and phone call privileges were extremely limited—all calls had to be made at the phone company in the center of the city, where the staff censored every call. No foreigner could visit the city, and citizens could visit for a maximum of only three days. Before traveling to the city, they had to obtain a permit, which was given only after an extensive background check.

When You Have a Truly Impossible Dream

At the time, the government forbade public assembly of any kind. That included all church services. So, no one could perform a baptism—public or private—or conduct a Communion service. Those caught holding a religious service would automatically be sentenced to a minimum of two years in jail. It appeared, then, that there was no way the dream could ever be fulfilled.

However, the women believed that religious freedom would come, because they firmly believed that because two of them had dreamed identical dreams, God was telling them something. So the women shared the dream with all the believers they met. These believers shared it with others, until the story of the dream had spanned the entire Soviet Union.

In 1991, I was asked to go to the Ukraine to preach the Adventist message. It was my privilege, along with my wife, Camille, and Max and Betty Trevino, to conduct the second evangelistic series to be held in that country after Gorbachev tore down the wall and introduced *perestroika* and *glasnost*. The Soviet Union was still intact. Gorbachev was still in power. Communism was still strong and restrictive. But we had a permit to hold public meetings and a field school of evangelism and to train pastors and church leaders from all over the country. I didn't realize it at the time, but Adventists all over the Soviet Union were aware of this series of meetings because of "the dream."

Toward the end of the series, Vitali Prolinski, the conference secretary, was sitting on the platform with me. During the announcements, he leaned toward me and said, through Leonid Drach, my translator, "We're seeing the dream being fulfilled right before our eyes." Something about the way he said those words told me he was speaking of a specific dream. Upon my questioning, he told me about the dream of the two women. He told me that during those days, he was a young minister who had to combine working and hiding. Leonid told me that he too had heard the story of the dream all his life.

These two men took our team to see Daria Sologub, one of the women who'd had the dream. She was old and infirm, lying upon her sick bed. But she was still alive. And she was very much aware of the current fulfillment of the dream she had shared with her friend Sister Pavlovna, who had since died. Every night one of the Ukrainian staff would record the meeting. Then someone would take the tape to her home, and she would listen to the gospel being preached in English and translated into Russian—and tears would roll down her cheeks.

In just three weeks, the Lord added 465 new believers to the small handful of members who had met in a converted house-church. Hundreds more were baptized in the weeks that followed, and when I returned six months later in the cold of December, more than a thousand people—most of them now members of the Adventist Church—gathered for a special Sabbath service. Two years later, Camille and I returned for a second series, and twelve hundred and fifty precious souls were baptized at the end of four weeks of meetings.

Others, including John Carter, have held meetings in Dnipropetrovs'k since that time, with similar results. There are now more than a dozen strong churches with more than three thousand members in an area where once there was just a handful of believers.

Just think, for forty-five years after the dream, there was little indication that it would ever be fulfilled. Just two years before we held our meeting, it was still illegal to conduct a baptism. Our pastors in the area showed us a place north of the city on the Dnieper River where the members would go and disguise their baptismal services as a swimming party and picnic. They did so knowing that if an informer had infiltrated their group, they would receive a jail sentence of at least two years for conducting a baptism. Even when we were there, we had to obtain a permit before the state would allow us to conduct the large baptism that closed our evangelistic meetings.

The next time you think there's no way out of a dilemma or predicament you're facing, remember the dream of Dnipropetrovs'k and hold on. Trust the Lord. Be patient and wait on Him, and in time you'll not only see the light at the end of the tunnel, but you'll also experience the beautiful warmth and openness that comes from leaving the tunnel altogether.

Keep on keeping on—even in the darkest of times. You'll be glad you did.

CHAPTER TWELVE

WHEN YOU LOSE YOUR HEALTH

A ll I know about my birth is what my mother told me—it was shortly after that event that my incredible memory kicked in! Mother said she was rolling out the dough for biscuits—probably using the same old Dr. Pepper bottle I saw her using later as a rolling pin—when I let it be known I was going to be born. I entered the world at 7:57 A.M., which means either they had very early breakfasts in those days or I was pretty quick!

I was the first of our family to be born in a hospital. My younger brother Paul was born there too. All three of our older siblings were born at home. Dr. B. H. Greer delivered me, as he had the older three. I guess he got tired of "home delivery" and changed to "take out"! Mom said she was afraid they wouldn't make it to the hospital in time, but aren't moms always worried about that?

I was born in October, just after my brother John had started the first grade. John was very healthy the first six years of his life; he had somehow avoided most of the childhood diseases: measles, mumps, chickenpox, etc. So, over the course of his first-grade year, he came down with most of these diseases and then brought them home to me. It wasn't the best way to start out—I was a sickly kid. Paul was just three years younger. He was strong and healthy, and when we dressed alike, people often thought we were twins, which really galled me. John was six years older and built like Tarzan.

To make matters worse, this very skinny kid, who could have been the poster child for a "feed the children" campaign, was stricken with polio at age three. By this time we had moved to Tyler, Texas. The epidemic was rampant, and the hospitals were full. You either lived or died at home. I thank the good Lord and Dr. Salk that a polio vaccine was developed, and I never had to worry about my children having this dreaded disease.

Fortunately, most of the damage I suffered was to a group of muscles on my left side, including my left pectoral muscle. While I was growing up, I was very sensitive about the way my chest looked. When I was at a beach, I would either wear a T-shirt or stand with my arms folded high so that my right hand covered the deformity.

When I was a child, my mother and my aunt Ora, her sister, would refer to me as "poor Jim." Aunt Ora was my favorite aunt, and her husband, Uncle Johnny, was my favorite uncle. My health must have been a topic of some of her conversations with her husband's relatives, because when they came to visit Ora and John, they wanted to see "poor Jim." At least one of them thought that was my name! That was a reputation I wanted to lose.

After supper one night, my mom and dad continued to visit at the kitchen table. Eating was certainly not a priority to me, and I was busy elsewhere in the house when Paul came to me, very concerned. He said Mom and Dad were planning to send me away.

Paul and I slipped into John's bedroom, which connected to the kitchen through a door that was usually closed to give him some privacy. We listened quietly as Mom and Dad continued their conversation.

"He's so skinny and sickly that he'll never be able to work or hold a job," I heard Mom say. "But he can sing pretty well, and I think this might just be the right thing for him."

Mom had read an article about the Texas Boys Choir in Fort Worth. The boys were brought in from all over the state and lived in a dormitory. They were trained in music and were also taught the regular educational curriculum.

Looking back now, I'm sure Mother was thinking ahead, trying to do what was best for me. She was trying to figure out how I could use my talent and develop my strengths so that my weaknesses wouldn't cause me to fail. But that's not how I took it then. I got the idea that they didn't think I could amount to anything, and that flat made me mad! That day I became a highly motivated kid. I promised Paul no one would separate us, and I determined to do something about my body.

Some of this motivation was healthy, and some of it was not. I was a big reader in those days. The librarian told me I had checked out more than nine hundred books during one school year. I didn't have the heart to tell her I didn't read all of them. I would pick several books I thought looked good, and when I got home I made my final choice. Still, I averaged one book a day.

I know some of you are saying, "Is he exaggerating?" No, I'm not. I must hasten to tell you that these weren't books on rocket science! They were more like the Hardy Boys series. I read all of those books at least once, and a host of others very much like them. I was also into my studies—so much so that my sixth-grade teacher at Birdwell Elementary, Mrs. Murdoch, nominated me to appear on the "Quiz Kids" TV show. Boy, did I have her snowed! She was a great teacher, and the prettiest one I ever had as well.

It seemed to me no one cared that I was the class intellectual—along with Larry Schoenbrun and Mike Khoury, with whom I competed. No, they liked Bobby McCreary, the class clown, and Sonny Haley, the best athlete in the school, and Bobby Dusek, the toughest guy in the class!

Bobby hated me for a variety of reasons—I'm pretty sure partly because his dad was a Church of Christ preacher. My brother Ed was dating a pretty girl who attended that church, but, while Ed wasn't an Adventist and he did go to church with her, he made it clear that he didn't believe Sunday was the biblical day of worship.

One day Bobby was chasing me at recess. He did this often. I was scared to death of him, but this time as I ran, the thought struck me that I couldn't run the rest of my life. I stopped suddenly, swung around, and hit Bobby as hard as I could right in the face! My swing, plus his momentum and my catching him totally by surprise accomplished a miracle. I won a one-punch victory over the all-time, undisputed champion of our class! Bobby was so groggy from that punch that someone had to help him up. I was too scared to stay around and was greatly relieved when the bell rang, ending recess. I felt a little like David whipping Goliath.

Bobby never asked for a rematch, and we became friends. After that, I determined that while I would never start a fight or be a bully, I would never run from a fight again if there were no peaceful way to avoid the confrontation. And I vowed that I would not stand by and watch someone bully someone else.

When you've been the underdog, it's not hard to take up for another underdog. One night when I was staying at a Holiday Inn in New England, a fight broke out in the hall just outside my room. I called the desk, and when I heard the manager yelling for the fighters to stop, I opened my door. One of the men who'd been fighting turned to attack the manager, who was one of the smallest adults I've ever seen. I stepped between them and told the man that he'd have to come through me first. He pulled back his fist, and I prepared for the worst. Then suddenly he thought better of it, turned around, and left.

The manager thanked me profusely, saying, "He would have killed me." Then he asked, "You know who that was, don't you?" When I admitted that I didn't, he told me that it was George Jones, the famous country singer who was also a famous brawler. I'd seen the bus parked out front with his name and Tammy Wynette's painted on the side, but I had no idea what he looked like.

Jones had just whipped his drummer and was ready to hurt the manager. I'm happy that my bluff worked and I didn't have to find out whether or not I could handle him.

The manager called my room later and said that Holiday Inn would pay my entire bill. I had been there for a couple of weeks and had eaten many meals as well, so that was quite a gift—worth the bluff!

That weekend, I met Camille and our children and her parents for church in Babylon, New York, where Jim Ripley was pastor. At the potluck after church, I met a friend of Jim and Maggie Ripley's, Arnold Cochran, who was sales manager for Bishop's Bakery in Cleveland, Tennessee. He looked at me and said, "You're the guy who backed George Jones down at the Holiday Inn in Fitchburg the other night!" I had no idea anyone else was watching, but at least it gave me a witness!

After the night when I heard Mother tell Dad her "boys' choir" idea, the focus of my life changed. I quit spending so much time with my head in a book, and I started eating foods I thought would make me healthier and stronger. I did everything I could to add weight to my very frail body. One of my coaches, Andy Woods, a legend in Tyler, once said to me, "Son, no matter how hard you try, you will never weigh more than 125 pounds soaking wet." Well, he was a great coach, but as a prophet, he was no better than my mother, who predicted I would never lose the nickname "Slim Jim." If you saw me now, you'd never guess that I'd been a frail child. I've certainly overcome in that area—perhaps more than necessary!

One of my coaches put me on a six-meal-a-day plan with several of those drinks the health food stores carry that are supposed to add weight. By the way, if you are thin, don't ever try to gain weight! Whatever you do, don't drink those "add weight" drinks. They won't work at first, when you really need them, but in about ten years they'll kick in—just about the time you wish you could lose some weight!

I also got involved in every sport I could. Instead of curling up in the living room with a book, I began to head for Mike Flowers's front yard, where I learned to play football and baseball in pickup games. Later, I joined the Apaches Little League baseball team. Eventually, I became a fixture at the baseball park where the minor-league Tyler Tigers played. There, with professional coaches helping me, I made great improvements as a player.

The manager of the team, "Salty" Parker, liked me and would let me shag balls in the outfield while the players took batting practice—something he let few others do. One day I asked Salty why he let me do this and not the others. I was hoping he would say, "Because you have such great potential as a player." Instead, he replied, "Because they steal balls and you don't." Whatever the reason, I appreciated the opportunity.

A few years later, Salty became the manager of the Dallas Eagles, part of the Giants organization. He remembered me, and when I asked for a tryout, he said OK. There were two great ballplayers on the field that hot June afternoon at old Burnett Field—Bill White and Willie McCovey. They were playing with the Dallas Eagles at the time; both of them later became Hall of Fame players. The cove in the old Candlestick Park in San Francisco, where Bobby Bonds often hit his home runs, was dubbed McCovey Cove after Willie. And Bill White became president of the National League after he retired as a player.

The day Salty gave a tryout to the kid he remembered from Tyler, the professional ballplayers razed me, as they did any would-be "rookie." I actually played way over my head that day. At the close of the workout, Salty signed me to a minor league contract. I was assigned to a team in a semi-pro league in Dallas—an "instructional league," in which professional players who had been injured and were trying to make a comeback and young players like me played. I did well on that team and finished the summer with the understanding I would go to spring training with the Giants the next spring.

When spring came, I made some decisions concerning my future, and my decisions didn't include baseball. I'd found something I wanted more. Would I have made it into the big leagues? Who knows? I asked that question of a friend who went to spring training that year. He was a catcher and had caught for me several times in games in which I'd pitched. He was a good guy; you could pretty much take his opinions to the bank. He told me I was better than most of the pitchers he caught there. He also said that spring they kept every pitcher who didn't develop a sore arm. So he felt I would have definitely made it to the minor leagues.

Would I have made it to the majors? Who knows? Would I have become a McCovey, White, Mays, or Mantle? No, I have no illusions about that! But I did get to play on the same field with two of them that day.

While I have no regrets about not pursuing that opportunity, sports were good for me. They helped me build a strong healthy body out of a sick one. And I learned teamwork—that people must work together to have success. I've worked with some people in my life who I wish had learned that important lesson. In baseball, you might want to swing away, but the coach may signal you to sacrifice bunt in order to advance the runner to second so he is in scoring position for the next hitter. You do what the coach wants for the team, even though you would like to try to hit the ball out of the park!

Do I believe people should push their kids into sports? No, absolutely not. Neither do I believe you should prohibit them from participating in sports. Is there danger in sports? Of course. There's also danger in hiking, rock climbing, diving, caving, camping, and many other activities. But this doesn't mean we shouldn't be involved in them.

What about the spiritual dangers in sports? As in any activity, there's the danger the game will become too important to us. I believed that if I wasn't willing to lay down baseball and leave it entirely alone during the hours of the Sabbath, I was making it my god and I was in violation of the commandment that says, "Thou shalt have no other gods before Me."

I never played a game on the Sabbath. Once, when sundown came during a championship game, I left the stadium and sat in a car, waiting for a ride home. No member of my family was attending that game; no one was urging me to come out of the game; and no one was there to take me home. It was summer, and the sun set late in the day. The game was nearly over. The coach urged me to play one more inning. I felt all the pressure to continue a person could ever feel, but I had promised God and my mom that I wouldn't play on the Sabbath, and I didn't.

In those days in our area, all the World Series games were broadcast on television as they were played. But the only other games that were broadcast were those played on Sabbath afternoon. Most of the members of our family were not Sabbath keepers, so they might be watching the baseball game of the week on television. But I would stay away from the room where the television was blaring. I truly felt that to watch a game would be putting baseball before my God. I felt I needed to keep everything in balance.

Do I think we should have competitive sports in our schools? Intramural sports, yes. I think the danger comes when we enter into intercollegiate play, where our schools play other schools that are not in our system. I'm not against giving scholarships for academics—for those preparing for ministry, teaching, or other majors that deal with humanitarian development. But I don't believe in athletic scholarships of any kind. However, I support all our schools, and I refuse to criticize any of them for trying to reach our young people or for the methods they use. I'm only expressing my personal opinion.

Sports dominate on the major state college campuses, and because of the royalties those schools receive from television broadcasts of their games, the sports are largely self-sustaining. However, many small colleges in America would like to eliminate their sports programs altogether because of the expense and the distraction they entail. Many schools have eliminated their league play and don't regret having done so. Perhaps we could learn a lesson by observing them.

Having gotten such a bad start with my health made me very thankful for the exceptionally good health I had for the next fifty years or so. The Lord gave me strength to carry very heavy schedules. For nearly half of those years I carried a full-time job in business and a full-time schedule in ministry on a self-supporting basis. During that time I had an occasional cold or the flu; otherwise, my health was outstanding.

However, during the summer of 1998, while I was president of the Arkansas-Louisiana Conference, I was under extreme stress, having to discipline two ministers. I also had a crusade in Kharkiv, Ukraine. When I returned home from Kharkiv, I was having symptoms that I couldn't ignore. I went to a gastroenterologist. After scoping me, he said I needed to eat more spinach.

The symptoms continued. I saw my personal physician and longtime friend Dr. Carl Markstrom and told him about my symptoms. I also told him I was concerned that I might have picked up a parasite overseas. While the wonderful people with whom I stayed had installed indoor plumbing, they were still using their outhouse, which stood only a few feet from the well that was the source for our drinking water. I used a filter, but they're not always 100 percent effective.

Dr. Markstrom wanted me to take a regimen of antibiotics, but I decided not to follow his advice, feeling I had taken too many antibiotics in my life.

Someone gave me a tape that featured a doctor who practiced natural medicine and urged me to see him. I did, and he ran some lab tests and showed me the results, which indicated, without a doubt, that I had a parasite. He told me he would treat me naturally and began a ninety-day treatment to "heat up" my immune system. At the end of the ninety days, the symptoms continued. I contacted him again, and he said we should repeat the treatment and increase the dosage.

The treatment apparently eliminated the parasite, but it either triggered or aggravated an autoimmune system problem I had. When the immune system gets out of balance, it can begin to attack otherwise healthy organs of the body. It treats them as if it were rejecting transplanted organs. My immune system had become too strong. The natural treatment had driven the system to such a high level that it was causing my body to reject itself. As a result, my colon was virtually destroyed. My system was poisoned.

I continued to work and didn't consult another doctor. Meanwhile, eating made me deathly ill. Eventually, Kenneth Cox, who was very concerned about me, got his daughter, Laura Becker, on my case. Laura is a nurse who's made a hobby of finding the best available physician and solution for unique medical problems. She found several physicians who were particularly qualified to deal with my problem. The one we chose was Dr. Mark Provensha, who was located right in Shreveport. By the time I got to him, it was nearly too late for him to do anything to help. He put me in the hospital, where I stayed for two and a half weeks. I hadn't realized how seriously ill I'd become.

Don Jacobsen came from the General Conference office and had an anointing service with a small group of pastors. And friends began to visit and call me. Orville Iversen was one of those friends. He called me every day. Orville and I had been especially close friends for about ten years. We shared many interests in ministry and had worked on many projects together. In one of those phone conversations, I said, "Well, Orville, don't worry about me. This illness is not life threatening."

He shocked me by saying, "You don't know, Jim. You could be much nearer to death than you think." Where he was getting his information, I don't know!

Dr. Markstrom came from Dallas to visit me on his day off. He sat with my chart for a long time, visited a little while, had prayer with me, and then left to make the two-hundred-mile trip back home. He told me later that he called his wife, Norma, and told her, "Jim's never going to leave the hospital alive. He's going down quickly." And then, he said, he cried.

When my friends would come, I could read their concern on their faces. Dale Brusett tried to hide his concern, but failed. When Jerry Mayes saw me, he became very worried and called the world-famous Mayo Clinic, trying to find a way to get me to there. Max Trevino, who had become president of the Southwestern Union Conference, called Art Nelson, the treasurer, and told him to have me flown to the Loma Linda medical center or to Florida Hospital in Orlando. And Cyril Miller, who was a general vice president of the North American Division, called and recommended that I talk to Dr. Ray Herber, who had just retired from Loma Linda University.

That was a great suggestion. We sent a copy of my hospital chart and test results to Dr. Herber so that he would know exactly what I was going through. When he read my file, his first words to me were, "You are a very sick man." I certainly agreed with that! He told me he had trained the heads of the gastrointestinal departments of both Loma Linda and Mayo, and he would recommend the same treatment I was receiving in Shreveport and so would they. Dr. Herber offered some dietetic suggestions that proved helpful in recovery. I appreciated his reassurance and his advice to forgo surgery at that time.

Through the entire illness, I continued to chair some committees. I really enjoyed working with our team. Being with fellow officers Don Upson, Gary Grimes, and Don Hevener brought me a great deal of encouragement.

Several of those meetings occurred while I was still in the hospital. One meeting was especially memorable. People were always call·
ing Camille and me with natural cures and insisting that we try them.
We were so desperate that we were willing to try anything! One of
those "cures" was raw cabbage juice. A little while before the conference officers came for a meeting, Camille arrived from home with
some fresh cabbage juice. I drank it down, and the men arrived for
the meeting.

A few minutes after we started the meeting, I began to get very
sick. My abdomen felt like it was about to explode. I began to belch
and perspire and was very ill. I bravely tried to continue the meeting,
but just watching me was bothering the other fellows. They finally
insisted, over my protest, that we end the meeting. Later, we laughed
about the meeting, and whenever we wondered about some decision
we had made, we would say we must have voted that at the "cabbage
patch" meeting!

I won't wear you out with a blow-by-blow description of my hos-
pitalization. Dr. Provensha finally told me he was going to give me a
couple of blood transfusions and then get me out of the hospital
before I caught something that would kill me! The doctors were
mostly concerned about pneumonia, because for eighteen days they
had been suppressing my immune system in order to heal my colon.

During that time, I contracted shingles, which in time developed
into the most painful illness I have ever had. I apologize for not ad-
equately sympathizing with those I have known who've also had severe cases of this disease, including my mother and H. M. S. Richards,
Jr. Anyone who's had shingles—especially when it wasn't treated soon
enough— knows what I'm talking about. No one recognized it in the
hospital in time for me to get treatment, which must be done within
forty-eight hours if it is to be effective. By the time they discovered
what I had, I was home.

The treatment didn't help, and I not only had a three-month bout
with the disease but also had post-herpetic neuralgia. This lasted
more than two years. The excruciating pain, much like third-degree
burns over a portion of your mid-section, continued night and day.
In the intensive first months, the pain would hit me in spasms much

like a kidney stone attack. It was so painful that I would nearly lose consciousness.

After a few days at home, I told Camille I wanted to go to the office. So, every day she would drive me there. I was walking with a cane and very weak. But, one step at a time, I would pull myself up the stairs to my office, which was located on the second floor. I would sit at my desk and try to work and then leave after a few minutes. One day while I was trying to work, one of the shingle spasm attacks hit me. The pain was so excruciating that I cried out. And even though I tried to muffle the cry, it was so loud that it scared people downstairs. I've never talked with anyone else who had shingles and said they had these terrible attacks. However, I talked with two emergency room physicians at different hospitals where I was taken when the pain wouldn't subside. They verified that they had treated these attacks before, and they said the attacks are more prevalent than most people realize.

On a flight from Dallas to Shreveport, one of these attacks hit me. We were sitting in the back row of a commuter plane. I put a handkerchief in my mouth to help drown out the cry. When the severe pain began to subside, I turned to Camille and said, "How did I do?" thinking she would praise me for suppressing the screams of pain that I couldn't stifle entirely.

"You scared the people on the plane half to death," she said. "The flight attendant has asked the pilot to land the plane at the nearest airport and put you off."

When the attendant returned from talking to the pilot, I assured her that I was fine now and would cause no further disturbance. Camille confirmed this, and the attendant told the pilot to continue on to Shreveport.

Shortly after I was out of the hospital, Max Trevino and Gary Grimes came to visit me and offered to take me for a drive. We stopped at a cell phone store where I knew the manager, and they helped me inside. I had a minor question for this manager, who had helped me with my phone many times. When he saw me, he turned and ran to the back of the store. It was a while before he returned. Later, after I recovered from my illness, he told me that when he saw me come in that day, he broke into tears and thought to himself, *Mr. Gilley is dying of something horrible.* He said he had to go to the back room to regain his composure.

In a few weeks, I felt that I could drive again and started doing so. My license was about to expire, so I went to the motor vehicle department to get it renewed. The clerk denied my request and said I had to bring a doctor's note stating I was physically able to drive. He arrived at this decision by looking at me, even though the woman in front of me was in a wheelchair and he had given her a license without question. I must have looked pretty bad.

Some humorous things happened during my recovery. On one occasion, Camille and I were waiting for a connecting flight at the Dallas-Fort Worth airport. (In my condition, I had no business continuing to make and keep appointments, but I did.) While we were waiting, I decided to get a shoeshine. When I got down from the shine stand, my legs gave way and I fell to the floor. I couldn't get up, so the attendant helped me, and I was very appreciative.

I had the exact amount of cash I needed to pay for the shine, but not enough change for a tip. So I went to a nearby stand and ordered two juice ices to get some change. When I returned, holding a glass in each hand, my pants fell down to my ankles. I thought everyone in the concourse was looking at me. Jaws dropped in amazement!

Camille arrived, and instead of taking the drinks so I could pull up my pants, she doubled over in laughter. When Camille hears a joke, she never laughs. But let something like this happen, and she loses control laughing! When I gave the shoeshine man the tip, he said, "You went to all of that trouble to give me a dollar?" I felt like asking him to return the tip. After that experience, I wore both a belt and suspenders. I wasn't going to take any more chances!

We went to Colorado for some meetings with the officers of the Southwestern Union Conference. We met every year, and I always looked forward to attending. When I left the hospital that year, I set a goal of attending this meeting. I was rushing things a bit. At the airport in Denver, I had to have a wheelchair, something I had to do several times when I faced a very long walk. Riding in the wheelchair embarrassed me, but it also gave me great empathy with those who have similar struggles. I discovered that no one ever looks directly at people in wheelchairs or smiles at them or speaks to them. Now, I try to speak to people in wheelchairs. Just a smile or a simple "How's it going today?" can at least let them know you acknowledge their existence!

The meeting was being conducted in Vail, Colorado. Most of the administrators were shocked when they saw me. It was the first time they'd seen me since my illness. However, the wife of one of the presidents kept telling me how great I looked. She was basing this on the fact that I had lost about eighty pounds, and less of me had to be an improvement!

Halfway through the first session, I needed to rest and went to my room to lie down. As I napped, I had the craziest dream. I dreamed an undertaker had come into the room and explained to me that I would really look good in my casket if they embalmed me while I was still alive. In my dream, I asked, "Is Camille in favor of this?"

"Yes," the undertaker said. "She wants you to look your best in the casket."

So I gave my permission, and he began the process. I was very relieved to wake up and find it was a dream! I told the president's wife about the dream, and I told her I would rather feel better and not look so good!

On Sabbath, we had a very special church service. During the prayer time, the entire group gathered around me, laying their hands on me as they prayed. Those prayers meant so much. When the sermon started, I could no longer sit in the pew. I had lost so much weight that I had no padding built in, so the hard pew was killing my bones. (I have a great sympathy for thin people who have to sit on unpadded pews; however, that's all the sympathy I have for them!) I went to the back of the chapel and sat on the one padded pew in the place. A man who was attending saw me sitting there alone. He came to the back of the room, sat down next to me, and gave me a genuine hug. I'll never forget that hug as long as I live.

A few minutes later, another person also offered sincere words of encouragement that I will never forget. He said, "Jim, a lot of people love you." I must say, that was news to me. I had never thought that was true before. Both of those men have suffered a lot. Those who suffer become more sensitive to the suffering of others. I wish both those men well.

While I was in Colorado, word came that my friend Orville Iversen had died unexpectedly after a short illness. I wanted so much to go to his funeral, but an emergency trip back to the hospital in Denver after the meetings were over ended that idea. I wanted Orville's son and daughter to know how much I loved him. He was a friend, an advisor, and more—he was like a surrogate father to me. Our entire family loved Orville; he was always welcome as a guest in our home. He was right when he told me that we never know how serious our illnesses might be.

Our mutual friend B. J. Christiansen was at the funeral. He was also fighting a serious illness. We were often in contact by phone or attending the same meetings, and we encouraged each other. A little over a year later we buried that fine, strong, young leader of the church. Now those two friends await, with so many others, the call of the Life-Giver!

The road back to health has been a long one. I'm still on the road, but I have made so much progress that when I look back, I'm amazed at how far I've come. I've experienced ups and downs, and I'll never be seventeen again! But I've learned that when we face a serious illness, we must hold on to Jesus. We mustn't quit. We must get the best medical advice we can find and follow it. But whatever we do, we should follow the admonition of James 5.

And we should follow that admonition right away! Some people think that anointing is the last rite. No, it should be the first rite! I don't think people should be anointed for a hangnail or a fever blister. But if you have a serious illness, have an anointing service with someone who believes that God answers prayer—especially when the condition or disease could be life threatening. I said to Dr. Provensha, my good doctor in Shreveport, "Thanks to you and the Lord, I'm still alive."

He replied, "You better reverse that order and thank the good Lord first, because I had done all I could and you were not responding to treatment. There was simply nothing else I could do." It was about that time that Don Jacobsen led an anointing and prayer service, and that's when I began to improve.

I believe we have the assurance that when we pray the prayer of faith and follow the admonition in James 5 to anoint the sick with oil, God will heal them. He may heal them immediately, or, as Scripture says, the sick may begin "to heal from that time forward," which is what happened to me. Or the healing may come in the resurrection, as will be the case of my friends Orville and B. J.

Actually, the last healing is the best of all, for it lasts for eternity, and the other two are only for a few years at best. But either way, our Lord guarantees our healing. "With his stripes, we are healed" (Isa. 53:5, KJV)—spiritually, mentally, and physically, forever!

So, keep on keeping on, even when you lose your health. There are better days ahead—I promise, because He has promised!

CHAPTER THIRTEEN

WHEN YOU LOSE A LOVED ONE

This chapter is one of the last ones that I wrote for this book. I put off writing it as long as I could. The grief I've suffered at the loss of loved ones is so personal that I find it very difficult to share. I know you understand what I am talking about; I'm sure you've had losses of your own—maybe more than I've had.

My wife has shared most of the losses that I will tell you about. She had five miscarriages, one of which was an infant son who was stillborn. However, she is fortunate to still have parents who are living and in good health. What a blessing they are to us and to our children and grandchildren. Our daughter Maryann, her husband Kirk, and their five beautiful children live next door to them. What a rich experience for those children to see their great-grandparents on a daily basis! And, I must add, what a joy for the great-grandparents, Pastor Roy and Venice Thurmon. Just yesterday my wife tried to call her mother. When she received no answer, she called Maryann, who informed her that Grandmother Thurmon was out in the new playhouse as a dinner guest of Katie, Camille, Grace, and Carrie! Great memories like that make for a great life for all involved.

I don't like funerals. I can't wait until the Lord puts an end to them. However, I did enjoy one. That was A. A. "Bishop" Leiske's funeral. I wasn't happy that he died. Quite the contrary; I had a great deal of respect and admiration for Bishop, as everyone called him.

After retiring from a full career of denominational service, he had developed a ministry and a nursing home empire that was very impressive.

The nursing home chain, which he built from the ground up, financed the ministry of *American Religious Town Hall,* his television program. It was a panel discussion program involving Roman Catholic, Jewish, and Protestant clergy. The panel also included a Seventh-day Adventist, the denomination to which Bishop Leiske belonged all his life. He served as the moderator of the program, which continues to be televised around the world—now, under the leadership of his son, Pastor Robert Leiske.

Bishop Leiske died suddenly one night after spending the day in a board meeting. That's how he would have wanted to die: with his "boots on," after a full day's work, having completed his agenda. The speakers at the funeral, which lasted several hours, were those who had served on the panel: ministers, priests, and rabbis, each telling a funnier story than the one before about life with the Bishop. He had lived a full and very productive life, and the large auditorium was filled with friends. He had no regrets and looked forward to the resurrection and life eternal with our Lord.

It's when the cycle of life is cut short that funerals become particularly difficult. I think of little Jason Forsburg, just four years old when he was struck by a car. To say that his parents, members of my church in Arlington, Texas, were devastated is a gross understatement. Pastors suffer not only their own tragedies but also, to a lesser degree, those of their members as well.

I've been experiencing the death of loved ones ever since I was seven years old, when our family had to bury my teenage sister, killed in an accident. My father was only fifty-eight years old when he died of cancer. Mom had a difficult time making it on her own after that; she had always been a stay-at-home mom. But she found a way to make a go of it and lived to the age of eighty-three. I've also lost several close friends, whose deaths have been almost as hard to live with as the loss of family members.

However, nothing has ever hit me like the death of Annie. She was born in Nashville, Tennessee, after a difficult pregnancy. My daughter Maryann had been taken there by ambulance from Dyersburg, in western Tennessee, where she, Kirk, and their children live.

Annie was a premature baby. The hospital where she was born was noted for having a great record at saving "premies." There were pictures all over the walls and bulletin boards of their successes. I longed for the day when Annie's picture would join them. I was just sure that would happen.

Annie had a great spirit about her. She was feisty. It was love at first sight. As I looked at her, I thought I saw little replicas of my feet and hands—though I knew she would overcome that and be beautiful someday! Her siblings, Katie, Ben, and Camille (named for her grandmother), fell for her too—as had her parents.

The whole family moved into one room at the Ronald McDonald House in Nashville, close to the hospital. Sometimes, some of the children would stay with us in Shreveport. They didn't want to be away from their mother, but they encouraged each other. I remember one day when little Camille was saying she wanted to go home. Ben told her, "We've got to do this for Annie."

All over the world, prayer groups had Annie on their prayer lists. I was very optimistic, especially as we neared the date when she was supposed to have developed enough to be able to go home. However, just two weeks before that date, Annie developed a problem with her lungs. Her condition very quickly became critical.

I was in Shreveport, still struggling to get well from my own long illness, when the call came. I drove to the airport and got on the next plane for Nashville. Before the door to the plane closed, my cell phone rang. It was my wife. Little Annie had gone to sleep in Jesus. When I hung up, the man next to me, sensing something was wrong, asked, "Bad news?"

I nodded and said, "Very bad." Then I told him what had happened.

I continued on to Nashville, went to the hospital, and met Maryann. She took me to the room where Annie was lying in her little casket, and we mingled our tears together. Annie had lived on this earth only four short months, but her death affected us all.

Maryann was so strong, her faith intact. She was already looking forward to raising Annie in the kingdom, after the resurrection.

Annie stayed in the hospital morgue that night, and the next morning, Kirk arranged for her body to be released for burial. Then the little casket was put in the car that I was driving. Kirk and Ben followed me in Kirk's pickup. And Maryann, my wife, Camille, and the other children followed them in another car. As I drove along, I thought about all that the undertakers do to help take some of the sting out of death. They pick up the body and prepare it for burial, and then we show up for the funeral and walk through the process. It is quite mechanical, and this relieves a lot of the pain. No one had lessened the pain we were suffering.

My daughter Maryann and her husband, Kirk Krueger, are a very industrious young couple. They are faithful in their support of the church and active ASI members, having run some of the children's programs at the annual convention for several years. They have great family values and are conservative Christians in their lifestyle, diet, and every aspect of their lives. This philosophy, their love for Annie, and their desire to be personally involved in every aspect of her burial were beautiful. It was touching and at the same time very difficult for all involved.

They had arranged for a private burial in a Civil War graveyard, the old Viar Community Cemetery. Kirk and my son John, who had driven over from Gentry, Arkansas, dug the grave. They finished just before sunset. Then we all made our way to the site. My father-in-law, Pastor Roy Thurmon, read some texts, said a few words, and then had prayer. Just as we were finishing, Kirk's sister Kathy and her husband, Dr. Lionel Meadows, arrived. They wanted to see little Annie, so the casket was opened again.

Katie, Kirk and Maryann's oldest child, understood what was happening and looked on quietly. But then the two younger children began to understand that we were going to leave Annie there in the grave. Ben had a very difficult time with this. He said, "What's wrong with you? Let's take her back to the hospital." As the casket rested on the ground next to the grave, little Camille placed her body over Annie's, hugging her and protecting her. That was one of the most difficult moments in our lives. Annie's death was so hard on the children—so hard on all of us! Oh, I know all about the Bible promises. They are beautiful, and I look forward to the resurrection. But death is difficult at best and devastating at worst. No wonder Christ died to put an end to it!

John 11:35, the shortest verse in the Bible, says, "Jesus wept." He wept even though He knew He would raise Lazarus in a few minutes. I think He still weeps when He sees your suffering and mine. Please don't think of Him as a faraway God, looking down from a long way off at your sorrow and tears. No, He is your Friend if you let Him be that to you—just as He was to Mary, Martha, and Lazarus. He is touched when you are hurting. Weeping is not a denial of faith. We don't weep as those who have no hope. Jesus wept and because He did, you can. You can also know that He is feeling your pain and wants to bring you comfort.

There are many places I would like to be on resurrection morning, but none more than right there next to Annie. I want to see her come to life perfectly whole. I want to see her placed in her mother's arms, a baby who will grow up in a perfect place that has no pain, disease, or death. God has promised just that—no more tears! Jesus said, "I go to prepare a place for you. And if I go and prepare a place for you, I will come again and receive you to Myself; that where I am, there you may be also" (John 14:2, 3, NKJV). What a promise!

Keep on keeping on, even when the world seems to crumble around you and hope is dim.

CHAPTER FOURTEEN

WHEN YOU FEEL LIKE THROWING IN THE TOWEL

You'll find that this chapter differs from the others in this book. I won't be telling stories from my life. Instead, I'm going to write a bit about depression. I'm doing so because depression successfully tempts too many people to give up rather than to "keep on" traveling the Christian road.—J. W. Gilley

Recently, at a large camp meeting, I delivered a message that I have preached many times, titled, like this book, "Keep On Keeping On." A woman came up afterward and said, "Oh, how I wish my sister-in-law had heard that message." She told me that only a few days before, this lovely young wife, mother, and leader in her local church had taken her own life. "I really believe if she had only heard this message, it would have given her hope to go on with life," she said.

I wish simple encouragement was all that was needed to keep someone from taking such tragic and drastic action, but in most cases it is not. Not when you are dealing with clinical depression. That's a condition that goes beyond mere discouragement. It's very important that, as Christians, we recognize depression in others and ourselves and know it is a condition that we must not take lightly.

Depression is a universal malady. A leading counselor said that he's traveled the world speaking on this subject and has never found anyone who hasn't experienced at least some depression. According to estimates, it affects 14 million Americans.[1]

Depression can be contagious. If you listen enough to negative people, it can rub off on you. As someone has said, psychologists, psychiatrists, and counselors who deal with problems all the time especially have to guard against depression. They're not immune.

Experiencing depression is not a denial of faith. Many noted Christians have suffered from this condition. Depression dogged Martin Luther, the great Protestant Reformer. He was depressed when he was in Rome, as he was crawling up Pilate's staircase on his hands and knees. The great truth that "the just shall live by faith" brought him spiritual renewal, but he still suffered from depression. After he nailed the ninety-five theses to the church door and translated the Bible into German, he still experienced depression. After he married Katharina von Bora, he still suffered depression.

Charles Spurgeon, probably one of the greatest of all preachers, said that he also suffered from depression. A man took down Spurgeon's sermons in shorthand, so we have them word for word right from the very beginning of his ministry. Everything that he ever said from the pulpit was printed. These records reveal that Spurgeon began many of his sermons by saying that he had battled with depression through the previous week and needed the prayers of the people. I submit to you that many other great spiritual leaders have had similar battles.

People who are depressed often can't do even the things that they would normally do on autopilot. Simple tasks seem complicated and exhausting. Depressed people experience changes in their sleep patterns. If they usually didn't sleep very much, they may start sleeping more and not want to get up in the morning. If they normally slept pretty well, they might start waking up during the night and find themselves unable to get back to sleep.

Depressed people may experience changes in their eating habits. If they've been normal eaters, they may suddenly lose their appetite or they may discover that they're constantly hungry and want to eat all the time. When they step on the scales and see that they've gained another pound, that in turn compounds their depression!

Or they may see a different crying pattern. Perhaps they've never really cried much at all, and now they start breaking into tears at the slightest provocation. Or they've cried quite easily, and now they can no longer cry. They may go to the funeral of a loved one and shed no tears. Or they may experience a loss of confidence or severe mood swings.

As in the case of illnesses like arthritis and heart disease, the symptoms of depression may vary widely from person to person. A combination of certain symptoms and signs helps doctors diagnosis the problem.[2] These symptoms include

- persistent feelings of sadness or irritability
- loss of interest or pleasure in activities that the person used to enjoy, such as hobbies or sex
- a change in weight or appetite
- sleep disturbances, such as trouble falling asleep, waking up too early, or oversleeping
- feelings of guilt, lack of self-worth, or helplessness
- decreased ability to concentrate
- fatigue or loss of energy
- either an increase or decrease in the person's normal activity level
- thoughts about life not being worthwhile or about suicide or death

For most people, the most frightening of these symptoms are thoughts of death or suicide. Having these thoughts does not mean the depressed person will act on them. However, it is important that he or she discuss these thoughts with a doctor. They are common symptoms of depression, just as fever is a common symptom of the flu.[3]

A person doesn't have to have all of these symptoms—or even most of them—to be diagnosed with depression. Most people have probably had some of the symptoms mentioned here when they weren't depressed, and the symptoms just went away spontaneously. It is the *persistence of symptoms* that is important to doctors in making the diagnosis of depression.[4]

Depression may have a number of causes. The depressed person may have been holding things in, failing to release his or her emotions. Imagine a company that manufactures a product and sends it to the warehouse for shipping. If the shipping department holds all the products rather than shipping them on, the warehouse would soon fill up. Then manufacturing line would have to shut down.

We have to release our emotions and not allow them to build up. Guilt, rejection, and anger can cause depression. I've seen people bottle up grief. They try to be stoic, thinking that's the way they're supposed to handle their pain. Then a terrible depression hits them, usually about a year after the death of their loved one. They haven't processed their grief properly. I recommend a grief recovery seminar for people who have suffered the loss of a loved one.

Or we may allow anger to build up because we've been told that as Christians, we're not to show anger. So what do we do? We repress our anger. Humorist Steven Wright says, "Depression is merely anger without enthusiasm." He's not far off.

The Bible says, "Be angry and sin not." In other words, it's normal to be angry—but we shouldn't do something stupid that we'll regret that will compound the situation. We should come to the place where we communicate our feelings as they arise. That way we can rid ourselves of anger a little at a time rather than waiting until we are full and then having it erupt all at once.

Sometimes we become angry with God. "God, I did exactly what You asked," we say. "I tithed, and I gave my offerings in addition, and my business still failed"—or "my health failed," "my house burned," or "my child died." That anger can become depression.

Aside from these faulty mental- and spiritual-health practices, however, doctors believe that, as in the case of diabetes and thyroid disease, a chemical problem causes depression. Neurotransmitters play an important role in regulating mood. Doctors believe depression results when something disturbs the functioning of these neurotransmitters. The resulting depression can be as disabling as arthritis, diabetes, or high blood pressure. It can prevent full participation in life.[5]

Clinical depression is not something we can take lightly. It's more than the "simple" or "normal" depression—the "blues" or the "blahs"—that all of us experience at times. People can't just snap out of clinical depression. It's not normally something they've brought on themselves, and it doesn't reflect a personal weakness or an inability to cope.[6]

I'm not a psychiatrist or psychologist; I'm a minister of the gospel. The counsel I give you is spiritual counsel that can help you with simple depression. However, if you had a broken arm, I would advise you to see a medical doctor. I would give you the same advice if you were persistently experiencing any of the symptoms listed above. Make an appointment with your personal physician. Either let your doctor treat you or get a referral to a specialist whom your doctor recommends.

Most often, only professionals can cure clinical depression. If you're "down" for more than a little while, you should see a physician. There are many good Christian psychologists and psychiatrists who believe in God and have faith in Him—they can be of great help. Under the care of a health professional, depression is very treatable. Proper tools in the hands of a believing, trained counselor can be very effective. Several kinds of treatments are available, including various types of counseling and psychotherapy. And doctors can prescribe several medications that restore the chemical balance in the brain.

It is important to remember that clinical depression is not something you can conquer with willpower or fix by just "pulling yourself together."[7] If you're fighting this battle, get the help you need to win it—to release your energy so that you can spend it on your loved ones and on traveling the road of life God has laid out before you.

As we look at the Bible, we find that depression is not something on which people of our time have a corner. God's people have always battled this plague. Numbers 11 contains a story about the children of Israel. They were complaining because they were tired of eating manna. There were only so many ways they could fix it. The Israelites were remembering some of the foods they'd eaten back in Egypt—

the fish, the onions, the garlic, and other spicy foods. They longed for those foods.

The Bible says, "Moses heard the people weeping throughout their families, everyone at the door of his tent; and the anger of the LORD was greatly aroused; Moses also was displeased" (verse 10, NKJV). The Hebrew word translated "displeased" can also be translated "distressed" or "depressed." Moses was upset. He said to the Lord, " 'Why have You afflicted Your servant? And why have I not found favor in Your sight, that You have laid the burden of all these people on me? Did I conceive all these people? Did I beget them, that You should say to me, "Carry them in your bosom, as a guardian carries a nursing child," to the land which you swore to their fathers? Where am I to get meat to give to all these people? For they weep all over me, saying, "Give us meat, that we may eat." I am not able to bear all these people alone, because the burden is too heavy for me. If You treat me like this, please kill me here and now—if I have found favor in Your sight—and do not let me see my wretchedness!' " (verses 11–15, NKJV).

Now that's depression! Moses was so depressed that he said, "God, please kill me. If I've found favor in Your sight, put me out of my misery so that I don't have to listen to these people."

Earlier, Moses had a similar experience. Exodus 18:13 says "the people stood before Moses from morning until evening. So when Moses' father-in-law saw all that he did for the people, he said, . . . 'Why do you alone sit, and all the people stand before you from morning until evening? . . . The thing that you do is not good. Both you and these people who are with you will wear yourselves out' " (NKJV). In this instance, I would say that we are looking at simple depression, as opposed to clinical depression.

Simple depression arises from several factors that may not require the help of a physician to resolve. First, you will normally discover that you're tired, run down, or totally depleted physically. You've been burning the candle at both ends. You've been trying to do too much. You're overextended. This was Moses' problem—he was doing too much. God remedied that. He told Moses to get "seventy men of the elders of Israel" to help him. God dealt with the cause of Moses' depression by lightening his load.

If you carry too heavy a load, you run the risk of becoming depressed just as Moses was. So, one remedy for simple depression is rest—lightening the load you're carrying or experiencing a change of scenery.

Second, there's often an emotional factor behind depression. Moses was angry with God. He was upset. He thought that God was not doing right by him. He thought God was laying this whole burden upon him, and he became emotional about it. Furthermore, the people didn't seem to appreciate him. He felt self-pity.

If you are angry with God, talk it out. Don't lie to Him. Tell Him you are angry, and tell Him why. Then listen to Him. This is a time for more prayer than usual. If your problem is not with God but with a spouse, teacher, fellow worker, or boss, get yourself in a proper mood by discussing the situation with a trusted friend or advisor. Then calmly talk it out with the person involved.

Third, there is usually a spiritual factor. We get so busy handling the details of daily life that we neglect fellowshipping with God. Moses felt the way he did because he thought God was neglecting him. Of course, the remedy is scheduling more time with God—or at least, spending your devotional time in a way that's helpful to you. Find the spiritual sources that best feed your soul with the positive things of God, that remind you of His love and care for you. Then make these sources a large part of your devotional life.

Christ and His disciples had a great time together on one of their missionary journeys. When they returned, He didn't say, "Let's go for another evangelistic campaign." The Bible says, "He took them apart for a season." Someone has said that if you don't go apart, you will come apart. A time of spiritual, physical, and mental renewal will usually bring optimism, enthusiasm, and genuine joy.

If you've followed these three suggestions and still are depressed, see a physician. You may have clinical depression.

Other biblical stories also picture depression. Let's see what we can learn from them.

The prophet Elijah had represented God so effectively up on Mount Carmel. He'd stood alone with great courage. God endorsed his stand by sending fire down from heaven to consume Elijah's sacrifice. Then the people destroyed the 850 prophets of Baal. When King Ahab started back for Jezreel, Elijah ran the whole twenty miles in front of his chariot, outrunning his horses. Elijah must have thought that when he arrived, another miracle was going to happen. Perhaps Ahab would be converted. Or maybe Jezebel would be converted, or someone would put her in her place. Perhaps Ahab would show some courage.

When Jezebel said she intended to see that Elijah was destroyed as the prophets of Baal had been, Elijah was frightened. He lost every bit of courage that he had, and he fled. He wanted to die.

As we look at the story, we see Elijah alone. He was physically exhausted after all that running. He had pushed himself to the maximum. He was emotionally down. He'd had such a high experience, and now the bottom had dropped out. One of the big problems with mountaintop experiences is that there is usually a corresponding valley. That's why we should aim at having a level experience with Christ.

Elijah was experiencing the dip that comes after a peak experience. That's simple depression time. Elijah had come to a spiritual crisis; note that he had concluded, "I am the only faithful one left." He had formed a martyr's complex. He was no longer seeing things clearly. God assured him, "You're not the only faithful one left. Seven thousand others have not bowed their knee to Baal." In this experience of Elijah, we see a perfect example of the physical, spiritual, and emotional components of simple depression.

What did God tell Elijah to do? He told him to go to sleep. When Elijah awakened, God fed him and told him to go back to sleep, and he did. Again, God woke him up and fed him.

There's nothing like good rest and good food. Too often, we try to exist on junk foods. Diet is very important in fighting off depression. God has blessed our church with the knowledge of how to maintain a good healthy diet. We need to use every bit of that knowledge.

When Elijah was restored physically, God gave him something to do—work therapy. He told Elijah, "I've got three things for you to do. Go to Syria and make Hazael king. Go back to Samaria and anoint Jehu king. Then find Elisha and make him a prophet with you." These were purposeful errands that involved a change of scenery.

Often, when we are depressed, we want to do nothing; we want to hide. In treating Elijah's depression, God gave him purposeful tasks to perform. When you are depressed, you need to stay active. Find projects that you can do that are not taxing emotionally. Make a list of productive errands and do them. Get out the "Honey do" list and get busy!

Jonah is another biblical example of depression. After his experience in the belly of the fish, he traveled to Nineveh, preached his message, and ended up exhausted. The people of Nineveh heard his message and repented. You would think Jonah would have been delighted about that. Instead, Scripture says, "It displeased Jonah exceedingly, and he became angry" (Jonah 4:1, NKJV). He became angry and "prayed to the Lord, 'Ah, LORD, was not this what I said when I was still in my country? Therefore I fled previously to Tarshish; for I know that You are a gracious and merciful God, slow to anger and abundant in lovingkindness, One who relents from doing harm. Therefore now, O LORD, please take my life from me, for it is better for me to die than to live!' " (verses 2, 3, NKJV).

So, first, Jonah was physically exhausted. Second, he was emotionally drained. He was overly concerned about his reputation. He was afraid some people would call him a false prophet. In addition, he was a bigot. He didn't really care for the people of Nineveh, and the fact that God was saving these non-Jews meant that they were equal with him, and he didn't buy that. Third, he was angry with God. He had a spiritual problem. Notice that again we see the three components of simple depression: the physical, mental or emotional, and spiritual.

The seven points that follow summarize what we can do about the milder form of depression:

1. Realize that depression is not sin. It's a symptom.
2. Maintain a regular program of rest and relaxation. We need to enjoy life, to laugh. The Bible says that laughter does good like a medicine. Going through life with a long face leads to a multitude of problems.
3. Take care of our physical health.

4. Guard against the subtle complexes that come along: the inferiority complex, the superiority complex, the martyr's complex. "I'm the only one who works around here" or "I'm the only one who cares."
5. Form at least one deep friendship with a fellow Christian with whom we can share our real thoughts or challenges.
6. Be glad for the success others experience, because jealousy, envy, and covetousness will always lead us to depression.
7. Remember that we are children of God. God loves us. He cares for us. When you are caught in a moment of despair, remind yourself that you are a child of the King. This will give you courage to fight whatever battle you are facing.

In 1956, a young Austrian sharpshooter entered the Olympics. In one of the shooting contests, he fired one hundred shots through the bull's-eye, winning the gold medal. Austria had not had many Olympic winners, so he immediately became a hero. He was paraded around the country.

When this sharpshooter returned to the factory where he worked, he was a bit rusty at his trade. While he was standing at a machine one day, someone startled him. He turned quickly, and when he did so, his sleeve was caught and his hand—his right hand, his shooting hand—was pulled into the machine. The machine mangled his hand so badly that it had to be amputated.

The sharpshooter came home from the hospital pale, thin, and shaking. He was also, understandably, depressed. He told his wife, "I can't stand this. I've got to do something about it." A few minutes later, she noticed that both he and his gun were gone. She said, "Oh, no," and ran out of the house, following his footprints in the snow into the woods. As she ran, she heard a shot. She fell to her knees, crying out, "Oh God, no. Please no."

Then she heard another shot . . . and another. Rising to her feet, she followed the footprints on into the woods. There she saw her husband holding his gun in his shaky left hand, firing at a target, and missing every time he pulled the trigger. Four years later, however, she sat in the stands and watched him compete in the Olympics. Once more, he won the gold medal—this time with his left hand!

God has gold for you, if you'll trust in Him. He wants to help you through every experience that you face. You may be facing something right now that you can't imagine holds anything good. It may have altered your lifestyle. Perhaps you've spent hours in agony, crying to God for an answer. I urge you to hold on to Him, to rely upon Him, to trust in Him. He will bring you that answer. He will bring peace into your life. I am amazed at what God has done for me. I am amazed at how He loves each of us equally, and I thank Him for His loving care.

So, keep on keeping on even in your darkest hour. I promise you that the sun will rise again!

1. See D. A. Regier, R. M. A. Hirschfeld, F. K. Goodwin, J. D. Burke, Jr., J. B. Lazar, and L. L. Judd, "The NIMH Depression Awareness, Recognition, and Treatment Program: Structure, Aims, and Scientific Basis," *American Journal of Psychiatry* (1988) 145:1351–1357.

2. See the *Diagnostic and Statistical Manual of Mental Disorders,* 3rd ed., revised (Washington, D.C.: American Psychiatric Association, 1987), 222, 223.

3. See ibid.

4. See W. Katon, "The Epidemiology of Depression in Medical Care," *International Journal of Psychiatric Medicine* (1987) 17:93–112.

5. See K. B. Wells, A. Stewart, R. D. Hays, et al, "The Functioning and Well-being of Depressed Patients: Results From the Medical Outcomes Study," *Journal of the American Medical Association* (1989) 262:914–919.

6. See ibid.

7. See Katon, ibid.

CHAPTER FIFTEEN

WHEN PROBLEMS COME

Life is a fantastic journey. It is a precious gift. Sometimes it brings unspeakable joy, and at other times indescribable pain. There are times when our souls soar like eagles, and there are times when we plunge into the depths of discouragement and despair. But through all of this, we have the joy and privilege of living.

In the sports world, people speak of the "thrill of victory and the agony of defeat." In the real world, we know both and have to learn to live comfortably with either. As I look at the problems that I've faced, the challenges and catastrophes that have come my way, I know one thing for sure: There will be more! I hope many more, because that will mean that I'll live a long life! To live is to have problems. Some are minor, and we handle them on a daily basis. Some are major. Knowing this, we should have a plan for handling major problems when they arise.

Careful living will avoid some but not all problems. I'll never have an automobile accident if I never drive or ride in a car. I won't die in a plane crash if I never travel by plane. However, restrictions like these would limit life too much for me. I need to fly to perform my ministry, but I don't need to fly in a private plane just for the fun of flying. I must travel by car for the same practical reasons, but I don't have to drive like a NASCAR driver or ride a motorcycle for transportation. I can be careful in my business dealings, mindful of contracts and agreements. I can avoid partnerships or business dealings with friends or relatives. I can list many "do's" and "don'ts" that will help me avoid problems—but I can't avoid all problems, pain, or difficulties. I can't live in a bubble. Even if I could, the bubble might pop!

So, problems will come. When they do, I must deal with them; few will go away on their own. Over the years, I've analyzed what to do when a problem comes. As a result, I've developed a simple, three-part plan of action. I call it "The Three Trusts."

First, trust the Lord. "Trust in the LORD with all your heart and lean not on your own understanding; in all your ways acknowledge him, and he will make your paths straight" (Proverbs 3:5, 6, NIV).

When we're facing a major problem, our first impulse is to focus on the problem. Don't do that. Instead, focus on the Lord. Most often, in such a situation, you'll have time to reflect upon a solution. It is very important that you seek God's will and ask Him for the strength, courage, and wisdom you'll need to face the problem. Thank Him that He has supported you in the challenges of the past and that He has brought you through each of them in His time. Along with most problems comes a blessing of one sort or another. Ask God to help you to find the blessing hidden in this problem, and thank Him for that blessing. Thank Him also for the closeness that you feel to Him when difficulties come and for Scripture's assurance that He is always with you and will "never leave you nor forsake you" (Joshua 1:5, NIV; Hebrews 13:5).

Be sure you trust Him explicitly for the solution and the timing. This is so important. We are often impatient with our praying. We expect to snap our fingers and to have an immediate solution. God doesn't often work that way. If you trust Him for a solution, He will give the solution to you. You must pray and think and wait on the Lord (see Psalm 27:14).

The Lord has the best solutions for the major problems you face. You must make sure you have His solution before you act. Test the solution with Philippians 4:8: Is it true, noble, right, pure, lovely, admirable, excellent, or praiseworthy? If the solution you are considering comes from the Lord, it will contain no deceit or dishonesty.

Second, trust your friends. If your friends are true friends and love the Lord, they want what is best for you. They can help you see the problem from a different perspective. Discuss the problem with a friend who is qualified to handle that particular problem. But you should also choose one whose loyalty to you and to the Lord is unquestionable.

Sometimes friends give counsel that is incomplete. However, their idea may become a part of the solution when joined with other thoughts that you've had. Don't depend on your friends for the entire answer, and don't tire them with the problem. That's a good way to lose your friends forever. You don't want them to dread seeing you coming or to start avoiding your phone calls.

I once knew a high-powered attorney. I couldn't afford his counsel, and we both knew it. We usually saw each other only in the lobby of the building where we both had offices. One day we went to lunch together. During lunch, I sought his advice, which he freely gave. When the check came, he said, "This lunch is on you. You pick up the check. You got enough free advice today to more than pay for lunch." After that, we made a deal. If I needed his counsel, I would take him to lunch. For the price of a lunch, I got a lot of good counsel.

That's not the only way to operate, but it is one good way. Going out for lunch keeps the visit short. Your picking up the check shows your appreciation and helps your friend a bit in return for the help he or she has given you.

Remember, while your problem may be the biggest thing in your world, don't wear your friend out with it. Do your best to be as upbeat as possible while you're searching for a solution. And remember, the final decision is still yours. Your friend may not know all the circumstances, so qualify the counsel he or she gives.

Third, trust yourself. If you are wise, you won't take this step first. However, after you've trusted the Lord, received the impressions that He gives, and have trusted your friends and their counsel, then it is time to trust the judgment and abilities that God has given to you. God does not want us to be weaklings. He wants to make us strong and give us genuine wisdom. He has promised wisdom to those who ask (James 1:2–5). For you not to move forward in confidence after you have taken the first two steps would be a denial of your faith that

He'll provide an answer. He wants to affirm you. He wants you to know that He loves you. He wants you to know that He has confidence in you.

We raise many of our problems by our own failures. If we've confessed those failures to Him, He has forgiven us for them (see 1 John 1:9). He wants us to forgive ourselves as well. He doesn't want us to keep heaping emotional garbage on ourselves for past or present failures. Paul said, "I can do all things through Christ who strengthens me" (Philippians 4:13, NKJV). God wants us to develop the kind of self-image that teams up with Him. You and I can be problem-solvers who can handle whatever He allows to come our way (1 Corinthians 10:13).

You may say, "I've messed up my life so much there is no way I can get things back on track." If Scripture contains one universal theme, it is the fantastic and almost at times outrageous grace of God. He offered it time and time again to the children of Israel, and He offers it to you and me today. There's a poem called "The Land of Beginning Again." It says,

I wish that there were some wonderful place
Called the Land of Beginning Again,
Where all our mistakes and all our heartaches
And all of our poor selfish grief
Could be dropped like a shabby old coat at the door,
And never be put on again.

I wish we could come on it all unaware,
Like the hunter who finds a lost trail;
And I wish that the one whom our blindness had done
The greatest injustice of all
Could be at the gates like an old friend that waits
For the comrade he's gladdest to hail.

It wouldn't be possible not to be kind
In the Land of Beginning Again;
And the ones we misjudged and the ones whom we grudged

Their moments of victory here
Would find in the grasp of our loving handclasp
More than penitent lips could explain.

Carl Bruin read that familiar poem, breathed into it life as it is found in Christ, and it came out like this:

I have found in the Book, that wonderful place,
Called the Land of Beginning Again,
Where the sins of the past are remembered no more
And the years, locust-eaten, the Lord doth restore.
All our filthy rags changed for a garment of grace,
And the soul is begotten again!

In that land only found by those mariners true
Who would follow the compass and chart,
We do note that the Lord against whom is all sin,
He who died on the cross our salvation to win,
We will find by the gate our best friend,
He still waits with a welcome for each seeking heart.

With a love shed abroad in our hearts by the Spirit,
It is easy to love one another;
That love thinketh no evil, it envieth not,
Is so humble—unselfish—with kindness so fraught,
That transformed by that love, as in Heaven above,
We shall love one another forever.

Oh, I wish, yes, I've found, that wonderful place
Called the Land of Beginning Again.

You *can* begin anew. The Bible says, "If any man be in Christ, he is a new creature: old things are passed away; behold, all things are become new" (2 Corinthians 5:17, KJV). Jesus came into this world to make us new. He is the only way to life eternal. If we come to Him and let Him have control of our lives, we can trust

Him entirely for life eternal a new life that begins in the present.

I believe that after we've settled the great question of our eternal destiny, we can face anything that life throws our way with assurance. When we know that God has given us eternal life, we know that He will certainly not forsake us in any way on this journey of life. Isaiah 43:2 contains His promise, "When you pass through the waters, I will be with you" (NKJV). Annie Johnson Flint took these words and expanded them in her magnificent poem "Passing Through":

"When Thou passest through the waters,"
    Deep the waves may be, and cold,
But Jehovah is our refuge
    And His promise is our hold,
For the Lord Himself hath said it,
    He the faithful God and true;
When thou comest to the waters,
    Thou shalt *not go down,* but *through.*

Seas of sorrow, seas of trial,
    Bitterest anguish, fiercest pain,
Rolling surges of temptation,
    Sweeping over heart and brain,
They shall never overflow us,
    For we know His word is true;
All [the] waves and all [the] billows
    He will *lead* us safely *through.*

Threatening breakers of destruction,
    Doubt's insidious undertow,
Shall not sink us, shall not drag us
    Out to ocean-depths of woe;
For His promise shall sustain us,
    Praise the Lord, whose word is true!
We shall not go down or under,
    He hath said, "Thou passest *through.*"

Not only does trusting God, our friends, and ourselves work for handling the problems that come our way in life, but it also will help us handle the loss of a loved one. If ever there is a time to turn to the Lord and to trust Him explicitly, it is at this time. At the death of a loved one, I expand the second step. As well as seeking the help of close friends during this time, I highly recommend that you turn to a professional whom you trust. The grief recovery programs offered in most communities are very helpful; you would do well to become involved in one of these. There you will meet other individuals who are suffering similar losses. They will become friends.

The third step is also vital. Those times of deep grief are also times to trust yourself. God has made you, He has sustained you in the past when you have had similar losses, and He wants you to dig deep within yourself for the strength that He has put there. Over the years, He has planted more strength deep within your soul than you may be aware of. All the passages of Scripture you've read, the prayer times you've had, and the experiences that God has brought you through have left a residue of strength and power on which you can call in difficult times. God wants you to face life and all its challenges with confidence.

Herb Doggette, vice-chairman of Walter Pearson's "Breath of Life" TV ministry, shared a story at our last board meeting concerning the making of the epic motion picture *Ben Hur*. Charlton Heston was the star of the classic film, and William Wyler was the director.

Wyler suggested that he thought the chariot race scene would be more realistic and have a greater impact if Heston drove one of the chariots—something a stunt double would normally do. After working for days with a trainer, Heston approached the famous director. "Mr. Wyler," he said, "I can drive the chariot well enough to race with the others. However, I don't know if I can win the race."

"Charlton," Wyler replied, "you stay in the race, and I'll make sure that you win."

My friend, that is what God is saying to you! You stay in the race of life with Him, and He'll make sure that you'll be victorious. You will win—Jesus Christ guarantees it!

Keep on keeping on!

If you enjoyed this book,
you'll enjoy these as well:

The Battle Is the Lord's
James W. Giley. Gilley offers spiritual strategies for victory in your daily struggles. Those strategies include five steps to overcoming unhealthy fear; four ways to deal with anxiety; and much more.
0-8163-1983-9. Paperback. US$10.99, Can$16.49.

Pilgrim's Problems
Karl Haffner. What are the problems of a modern-day pilgrim? Haffner uses Bible stories, humor, and modern anecdotes to help today's Christian deal with anger, loss, resentment, guilt, pride, greed, and other barriers to godliness.
0-8163-2022-5. Paperback. US$11.99, Can$17.99.

Let Not Your Heart Be Troubled
Randy Maxwell. Filled with personal illustrations, this unique sharing gift book is comforting reading for anyone grappling with worries about terror, death, God's love for them, the end, and more. This book helps the reader cling to Jesus in the storms of life.
0-8163-1915-4. Hardcover. US$9.99, Can$14.99.

Order from your ABC by calling **1-800-765-6955**, or get online and shop our virtual store at **www.AdventistBookCenter.com.**

· Read a chapter from your favorite book
· Order online
· Sign up for email notices on new products

Prices subject to change without notice.